Praise for *52 Secrets for Goal-Setting and Goal-Getting*

"Allow *52 Secrets for Goal-Setting and Goal-Getting* to give you what you need—whether it's a gentle nudge or huge push—to take action in creating the life you desire."

—Brian Tracy, author of the bestselling book *Eat That Frog*

"Deb Eckerling has many talents, but one of them is gathering the most interesting and 'achieving' people around, and distilling their success secrets for all of us. Prepare to have your butt kicked into getting what *you* want for your life by the gosh-darn-nicest coach around!"

—Rob Kutner, Emmy-winning writer for *Conan* and *The Daily Show with Jon Stewart*, and author of *Snot Goblins and Other Tasteless Tales* and *Look Out for the Little Guy*, the "in-universe" memoir of Scott "Ant-Man" Lang.

"The business world is a smorgasbord of companies, products, and ideas. Debra Eckerling's book brings these all together, with the goal of sharing the 'secret sauces' that flavor success."

—Noah Bleich, founder of The Teabook

"I live by the rule of 'Yeah, Why not?' I use that mantra to try new things, even if I'm not sure what the outcome will be. I love how Debra gathers people from all walks of life to share what works for them. She does this beautifully on her GoalChat podcast, as well as in this book. Do yourself a favor: 'Why not' give *52 Secrets for Goal-Setting and Goal-Getting* a try?"

—Annie Korzen, actor, TikTok star, and author of *The Book of Annie: Humor, Heart, and Chutzpah from an Accidental Influencer*

"While I totally think *52 Secrets for Goal-Setting and Goal-Getting* is a book that can be picked up and put down, I couldn't put it down! I kept wanting to know one more nugget, one more idea! The fascinating thing about Deb Eckerling's new book is that not only is it a guidebook that provides concrete, actionable steps for achieving one's goals, but it also provides these actionable steps from a diverse set of accomplished individuals. And it is in this diversity of talent that you have an opportunity to find what clicks for you! Deb's ability to bring together this wide variety of thought leaders across so many different disciplines makes for a truly informative and engaging read."

—Beth Ricanati, MD, award-winning author of *Braided: A Journey of a Thousand Challahs*

"How perfect that Deb Eckerling's new book has exactly 52 amazing tips to help you zero in on your goals and then masterfully achieve them. That means for the next year, just once a week, you can spend just two or three minutes to up-level your achievement game like a badass boss. I'm *so* in."

—David H. Lawrence XVII, actor/audiobook narration coach

"In successful goal-setting, there is no one-size-fits-all pathway that's perfect for everyone, and Debra Eckerling celebrates the reality that different people require different processes. She deftly illustrates the immeasurable value in sampling the many methodologies of a diverse array of achievers in far-flung fields, providing insight, inspiration, and motivation to adopt what feels right for you."

—Scott Huver, entertainment reporter
and author of *Beverly Hills Noir*

"One of Deb's superpowers is bringing together brilliant people to create valuable dialogue. She lifts everyone up, is generous with her knowledge, and her spirit is easily seen in the pages of this brilliant book!"

—Leisa Reid, founder of Get Speaking Gigs Now
and CEO of The International Speaker Network

"Debra Eckerling's *52 Secrets for Goal-Setting and Goal-Getting* is a vibrant and practical guide packed with actionable insights from an impressive range of people. Her unique blend of strategic foresight and hands-on advice makes this book an indispensable resource for anyone ready to move from dreaming to doing. It's as energizing as it is empowering."

—Jillian Vorce, author of *20/20 Mind Sight* and founder of The Jillian Group and One Handshake

"Deb Eckerling has a knack for getting people to reveal their truest selves. I'm struck by how she's gotten all these accomplished, successful people to reveal down-to-earth, very relatable sides...so that when each one offers a secret for success, every one of those secrets feels like something I can do today!"

—David Chiu, marketing & communications manager for The Braid

"Creating any life plan begins with role models. 'If you can see it, you can be it.' Debra Eckerling's sage advice is laced together with stories of real-life people who vaulted over life's sometimes unimaginable obstacles to achieve success. Make your own patchwork quilt from a combination of these helpful vignettes. Your future awaits you."

—Dr. Wendy Walsh, America's relationship expert and host of *The Dr. Wendy Walsh Show* on iHeart Radio

"*52 Secrets for Goal-Setting and Goal-Getting* is a game-changer for anyone serious about achieving their dreams. Debra Eckerling's knack for extracting powerful, actionable advice from top experts makes this book a must-read. It's packed with practical tips that you can start using immediately to stay focused, grow your network, and get more done. It's like having a personal coach cheering you on every step of the way!"

—Erik Fisher, host/producer of *Beyond the To-Do List* podcast

"We all need a cheerleader, but even more crucial is having that support from those who have been, as the story goes, 'in the arena.' Real experiential inspiration lands differently. What Debra Eckerling has done with this wonderful book is provide the reader with examples that have worked. Short and insightful, each entry is a powerful way to learn and in some cases, adapt or adjust strategy."

—Yael Swerdlow, MPD, CEO/founder of Maestro Games, SPC

"I love the upbeat tone, along with the range of actionable advice, in Debra Eckerling's *52 Secrets for Goal-Setting and Goal-Getting*. As a busy mom, keynote speaker, home design TV personality, and real estate agent, I am constantly juggling my personal and professional responsibilities. Whether you strive for work-life balance, a flourishing career, or a booming business, there's something in Debra's book that will speak to you. It's a must-read! I loved it!"

—Tanya Memme, keynote speaker, award-winning home design TV host, and real estate professional

"As a chef and entrepreneur who has navigated the bustling worlds of food trucks, restaurants, and catering, I know the importance of practical advice and innovative strategies in achieving professional success. *52 Secrets for Goal-Setting and Goal-Getting* by Debra Eckerling is a treasure trove of insightful tips that resonate with anyone looking to elevate their business or personal goals. Debra's book offers clear, actionable steps that are easy to integrate into your daily routine, enhancing productivity and inspiring growth. Whether you're a seasoned professional or just starting out, this book is a must-read for harnessing your potential and crafting the career you desire."

—Daniel Shemtob, all-star winner of Food Network's *The Great Food Truck Race*, the chef behind downtown LA's HATCH yakitori, author of *Food Truck Mogul*, and co-founder of Snibbs

52 SECRETS
FOR GOAL-SETTING AND GOAL-GETTING

Also by Debra Eckerling

Your Goal Guide: A Roadmap for Setting, Planning and Achieving Your Goals

Write on Blogging: 51 Tips to Create, Write, and Promote Your Blog

Purple Pencil Adventures: Writing Prompts for Kids of All Ages

52 SECRETS FOR GOAL-SETTING AND GOAL-GETTING

How to Stay Focused, Grow Your Network and Get More Done in Less Time

DEBRA ECKERLING

mango PUBLISHING
MIAMI

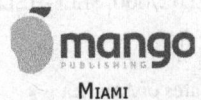

Copyright © 2025 by Debra Eckerling.
Published by Mango Publishing, a division of Mango Publishing Group, Inc.

Cover Design & Layout: Roberto Núñez
Author Photo: Dave Johnson

Mango is an active supporter of authors' rights to free speech and artistic expression in their books. The purpose of copyright is to encourage authors to produce exceptional works that enrich our culture and our open society.

Uploading or distributing photos, scans or any content from this book without prior permission is theft of the author's intellectual property. Please honor the author's work as you would your own. Thank you in advance for respecting our author's rights.

For permission requests, please contact the publisher at:
Mango Publishing Group
5966 South Dixie Highway, Suite 300
Miami, FL 33143
info@mango.bz

For special orders, quantity sales, course adoptions and corporate sales, please email the publisher at sales@mango.bz. For trade and wholesale sales, please contact Ingram Publisher Services at customer.service@ingramcontent.com or +1.800.509.4887.

52 Secrets for Goal-Setting and Goal-Getting: How to Stay Focused, Grow Your Network and Get More Done in Less Time

Library of Congress Cataloging-in-Publication number: 2024946737
ISBN: (print) 978-1-68481-717-7, (ebook) 978-1-68481-718-4
BISAC category code SEL027000, SELF-HELP / Personal Growth / Success

Printed in the United States of America

In loving memory of my mom, Arlene Leder.

Everything I know about kindness, cheerleading/uplifting others, and community I learned from her. Mom taught me the value of a conversation, the importance of following your passion, and so many other things.

I am forever blessed!

TABLE OF CONTENTS

14	**Foreword**
17	Introduction: The Secret to Success Is There Is No One Secret
23	**Part 1 - Focus**
24	Chapter 1: Figuring Out What You Don't Want Is as Important as Knowing What Lights You Up
28	Chapter 2: Visualization Is Magic
32	Chapter 3: Have Purpose Behind Your Plans
35	Chapter 4: Harness the Power of Color
38	Chapter 5: Commitment Drives Everything
41	Chapter 6: Endurance and Perseverance
45	Chapter 7: Follow the Five Ps
48	Chapter 8: Preserve Time to Nurture Your Business
51	Bonus Chapter: Use Your Superpowers to Create a Life Full of Impact
55	**Part 2 - Well-Being**
56	Chapter 9: Seek Harmony, Not Balance
59	Chapter 10: Stand Up! It's Harder Than It Sounds
62	Chapter 11: Listen to Your Body. Your Body Knows Everything.
65	Chapter 12: Energy Management
69	Chapter 13: Be Honest with Yourself
72	Chapter 14: Think Positively and Believe in Yourself
74	Chapter 15: Remove the Roadblocks
77	Bonus Chapter: Worrying Is a Waste of Time
80	**Part 3 - Action**
81	Chapter 16: It Always Pays to Reach
86	Chapter 17: Go with Your Gut
89	Chapter 18: Be Prepared and Be Kind
91	Chapter 19: Treat People Like Family
93	Chapter 20: Be Able to Look at Yourself in the Mirror
96	Chapter 21: Know Your Stuff
99	Chapter 22: Never Dream Harder Than You Work
102	Chapter 23: Be Ready!
105	Bonus Chapter: Just Go
108	**Part 4 - Networking**
109	Chapter 24: Leverage Your Network's Network
113	Chapter 25: Attend Networking Events with a Plan
116	Chapter 26: Commit to Conversations
119	Chapter 27: Find the Whos for Your Hows

122	Chapter 28: Begging Never Helped a Relationship
125	Chapter 29: Use "Windows," Not "Doorway," Thinking
128	Chapter 30: Visibility = Opportunity
130	Bonus Chapter: Create Your Own Community

133	**Part 5 - Communication**
134	Chapter 31: Be Able to Say What You Do in Three Words
138	Chapter 32: Preach What You Practice
141	Chapter 33: Be Unapologetically Yourself in All Aspects of Your Business
143	Chapter 34: Shining Brightly
145	Chapter 35: Think Big in Your Media Outreach
149	Chapter 36: Underpromise and Overdeliver in Any Media Situation
152	Chapter 37: Remember Hanlon's Razor
154	Chapter 38: Add Your Personality and Spin
158	Bonus Chapter: Effective Communication Is About Feeling, Not Thinking

161	**Part 6 - Productivity**
162	Chapter 39: Paper for Productivity
165	Chapter 40: Wear One Hat at a Time
168	Chapter 41: Baby Steps Every Single Day
170	Chapter 42: Lists, Batching, and Boundaries
172	Chapter 43: Give Yourself a (Lunch) Break
174	Chapter 44: Schedule Time to Work
176	Chapter 45: Calculate the Consequences
179	Bonus Chapter: Catalog Your Ideas

182	**Part 7 - Leadership and Teamwork**
183	Chapter 46: Let Your Team Know They Matter
186	Chapter 47: Managing Down Is as Important as Managing Up
189	Chapter 48: Mentor Your Replacement
191	Chapter 49: Seek Alignment
194	Chapter 50: Understand the Business Side of Your Creative Process
199	Chapter 51: The Buddy System
201	Chapter 52: Successful Projects Are a Combination of Hard Work, Creativity, and a Positive Attitude
204	Bonus Chapter: Sustainability First, Scalability Second
206	Conclusion: What's Your Secret?
208	Afterword: Embrace the Grit Mindset
210	Appendix A: Learn More About...
215	Appendix B: What Is the DEB Method?

230	**P.S.: Thanks for Reading**
232	**Acknowledgements**
233	**About the Author**

FOREWORD

You are in charge of your own destiny.

If you are not living the life you want, you have the power to change it. If you are ready to level up your business or career, *52 Secrets for Goal-Setting and Goal-Getting: How to Stay Focused, Grow Your Network and Get More Done in Less Time* is the book for you.

With advice from authorities in a variety of fields, from business and tech to food and entertainment, *52 Secrets for Goal-Setting and Goal-Getting* gives you the words of wisdom you need, exactly when you need them. These are proven practices from successful people, including Guy Kawasaki, "the Queen of Facebook" Mari Smith, and producer and author Arthur Smith (*Hell's Kitchen*), sharing what has worked for them.

One of Debra Eckerling's gifts is the ability to bring people who would not normally meet together in conversation. She has done this through her *GoalChat* live show and podcast for the last several years. Another talent is inspiring action through simple strategies. Debra's first book, *Your Goal Guide: A Roadmap for Setting, Planning and Achieving Your Goals,* does something most books skip over: it helps you figure out what it is you really want before offering advice and insight on how to turn your ideal life into reality.

52 Secrets for Goal-Setting and Goal-Getting brings you best practices of leaders, entrepreneurs, writers, producers, actors, chefs, and so many others. Let their voices, energy, and experience guide you.

In my book *Eat that Frog! 21 Great Ways To Stop Procrastinating And Get More Done In Less Time*, I tell readers to start their day with the biggest, most important, and most dreaded task. If your day is full of dreaded tasks, if you procrastinate more than you accomplish, if you are not utilizing your highest-value skills in a significant way, then it may be time to reevaluate your path and your purpose.

The first tip in *Eat that Frog!* is to "Set the table," a.k.a. figure out your goals. Know where you want to go, find out how to get there, and make progress on a regular basis.

Every day, you make thousands of decisions, from what to wear and what to eat to where to go and what to do. However, one conscious decision you can and should make every day is to live a good life…one with purpose that makes you happy.

Allow *52 Secrets for Goal-Setting and Goal-Getting* to give you what you need—whether it's a gentle nudge or huge push—to take action in creating the life you desire.

Brian Tracy is chairman and CEO of Brian Tracy International. As a keynote speaker and seminar leader, he addresses more than 250,000 people each year. He is the bestselling author of more than 80 books that have been translated into dozens of languages. He has served as a consultant and trainer to over 1,000 corporations and more than 10,000 medium-sized enterprises in more than 75 countries. He lives in Solana Beach, California.

INTRODUCTION:

The Secret to Success Is There Is No One Secret

Discover what works for others, figure out which of their strategies you can incorporate into your life, and carve out your own path.

I love helping people set goals that position them for success, *and* giving them the inspiration, motivation, and resources they need to achieve them.

My first goal-setting book, *Your Goal Guide: A Roadmap for Setting, Planning and Achieving Your Goals*, is designed to help busy professionals embrace change by choice or circumstance. It came out in January 2020…six weeks before the whole world experienced change via circumstances.

One of the blessings—yes, blessings—that came out of the pandemic was the ability to connect and develop relationships with others, no matter where they were in the world. Of the experts, professionals, and leaders I interviewed for this book, I have met fewer than a quarter in person. Still, some have become my closest friends.

I started my *GoalChatLive* show—also the *GoalChat* podcast—in 2020. Every week, I bring together three guests to dive into a professional or personal topic. In most cases, my guests have not met prior to sharing the virtual stage. The result is typically an engaging, informative conversation where everyone benefits, including the guests. Friendships are made, and it always makes me happy, when I see their collaborations—be it a joint project or guesting on each other's podcasts—come up in my social media feed.

My journey into the realm of goal-setting started nearly thirty years ago, when I established a writers' support group at Barnes & Noble in Schaumburg, Illinois. I saw firsthand the transformative power of goal-setting, productivity, and community. *I would never ask anyone to do something I would not do myself, so I would set and accomplish goals along with everyone else.*

After relocating to Los Angeles, I reinitiated my goals group at Barnes & Noble in Santa Monica, where it subsequently received the moniker Write On. The group, which started in 2002, has grown and evolved over time to encompass a diverse set of creatives and entrepreneurs, as well. These days, its primary home is the Write On! Online Facebook group (Facebook.com/groups/WriteOnOnline), which has been on The Write Life's "Best Facebook Groups for Writers" list since 2016.

As a result of leading the group, and in concert with my professional background in project management and communications, I began helping individuals identify, plan, and accomplish their business and project goals. I started speaking at events and leading workshops. After years of adapting and polishing my goal-setting and productivity techniques, I turned it into a simple system called *the* D*E*B METHOD©. More on that in Appendix B.

During client meetings and workshops, I would ask about their goals for the year/season/immediate future. Then, I would add, "What practices are you going to put in place to make sure they get done?" This could be anything from dedicated time each week to work on their passion project and sending out queries to scheduling "to-do list" time or establishing a reward system.

When we identify and embrace strategies that enable us to be more focused and productive, it speeds up our progress, improves our output, and even makes us happier. You don't have to love your career/job/business 100 percent of the time. However, when you have things in your life that bring you joy, that energy can uplift you and keep you moving forward.

Over the years, I have had numerous conversations with clients, peers, and friends about the power of creating strategies that set you up for success. In the fall of 2023, after a conversation with my publisher, Brenda Knight, about how simple rules can make a huge difference, this book started to take shape. Brenda is a huge fan of "No-Email Mondays" (more accurately, "No emails that require action items on Monday, because I am busy catching up on all the emails and work that came in over the weekend"), and I value my regular "Zoom-Free Fridays" (having one meeting-free day each week, which isn't necessarily on Friday, increases productivity and focus).

Thank you, Brenda, for giving me the opportunity to turn an idea that I feel very passionate about into an all-in-one resource, containing philosophies, methodologies, and best practices from those who have achieved success.

Who Is Featured in the Book

52 Secrets for Goal-Setting and Goal-Getting brings together value-driven humans who genuinely want to help others improve their lives. When reaching out to entrepreneurs, educators, consultants, creatives, chefs, writers, thought leaders, and other professionals to interview, I was greeted with enthusiasm. They were excited to impart their favorite words of wisdom.

I am also proud to say that everyone who contributed tips is either someone I interviewed for an article or on a podcast, a friend, a friend of a friend, or more than one of the above. My requirements for inclusion were simple: good person, good energy, and someone I would be friends with.

What's in the Book

52 Secrets for Goal-Setting and Goal-Getting is divided into seven sections:

- Focus

- Well-being
- Action
- Networking
- Communication
- Productivity
- Leadership and Teamwork

Each secret includes a description, example and/or anecdote, and information about the person who is sharing it. Some tips are short and direct, others are more detailed. All are valuable. Plus, there is a bonus secret in every chapter. If you'd like to learn more about those featured in the book, their websites/preferred links are listed in Appendix A.

Many of the tips could be categorized in more than one section. For instance, communication is a big part of networking. Things that help you focus can also improve your well-being. Leadership, teamwork, and action go hand in hand. And many productivity tips are relevant to other areas.

- Do you need a new strategy, motivation, inspiration, or all of the above?
- Are you building a business or career, or pursuing a passion project or thought-leadership status?
- Are you seeking a healthier or more balanced life?

You *could* read this book start to finish. Or you can also go directly to the section or advice you need to hear.

Let *52 Secrets for Goal-Setting and Goal-Getting: How to Stay Focused, Grow Your Network and Get More Done in Less Time* help you build the successful life you desire and deserve!

PART 1 -

FOCUS

Get clear on your aspirations, and then move forward with energy and determination.

CHAPTER 1:

Figuring Out What You Don't Want Is as Important as Knowing What Lights You Up

PATRICK J. ADAMS

Ever since I was a kid, I would get energized whenever I went to see plays and films. I'd come home inspired, thinking, "How did they do that?" "Why do I feel this way?" "Why do I want to see it again?"

While I don't do a lot of really clear manifesting, I know that whenever I go where my spirit tells me, 100 percent of the time I end up somewhere interesting and rewarding. I've learned, I've grown, I've found success.

And when I'm going in a direction that *does not* feel right, I know that instantaneously too. Finely tuning that instrument, and learning to trust my intuition more, is something I've gotten better at over the years.

Right before I got *Suits*, I had an experience that was the clearest example of being on the wrong path.

I was an actor. I was a desperate actor. I was a scared actor. And I was an actor who had no business being picky about opportunities. You take what you can get and, if you can get the audition, you go. But that was always really hard for me, because I had a very clear idea of the kind of work I wanted to be doing; I felt I knew where I was strong and where I wasn't.

I got an audition for this half-hour sitcom pilot, which was not my strong suit. I don't watch a lot of sitcoms, and I didn't think that I was meant for it. But my team was like, "You gotta go. This is really good. It's the big one. You should really be excited about it."

I was too young to draw a clear boundary for myself, so I just went. I remember thinking, "I won't do well, and it'll just be another bad audition."

But the director saw something in me and got really excited. He brought me in a couple of times through the audition process: callbacks, the director session. All of a sudden, I'm testing for this thing that I know I don't like. The script wasn't funny and I knew I couldn't make it funny. I didn't want to say that I was not the right guy for the role, so I kept going. And I got the job.

The table read—with the actors, the team, and all the executives—was a disaster! Not a single laugh was had. I was nervous and uncomfortable. It was awful.

When I got home, I got a phone call from the director. "The network is worried," he said. "But I want to shoot some scenes with you; we're going to prove them wrong." We didn't.

Two days after we shot those scenes, I got the phone call that I was fired. It was big news in the entertainment trades; it just felt very humiliating to this young insecure actor. I felt so pathetic; I was sure it was the end of my acting career.

Three months later, I got the script for *Suits*.

I don't regret anything. Everything happens for a reason. If that sitcom disaster happened just to tee me up for *Suits*, then I was okay with it.

After I read the *Suits* script, I went, "This is it! This is my show." I had no doubt that I could say those words and mean them.

I knew I might not get this part. But I also knew that I could—and would—crush this audition and have fun doing it.

To go from being publicly fired from a show I had no business auditioning for to a role that became successful beyond my wildest imagination was a huge moment of contrast.

I know I'm incredibly blessed. I am lucky to have such a successful career in an insanely difficult industry. I knew *Suits* was my role as clearly as I knew the other one was not for me.

I knew I belonged there. I had earned my place at that table, and I was excited to do that work.

> For seven seasons, Patrick J. Adams charmed audiences worldwide as Mike Ross in USA's hit drama *Suits*, a role which garnered him a Screen Actors Guild Award nomination. Most recently, Adams led the CBC limited series *Plan B* and made his Broadway debut in Richard Greenberg's Tony Award-winning revival of *Take Me Out*. He also starred as original Mercury 7 astronaut John Glenn in National Geographic's first scripted series for Disney+, *The Right Stuff*. Additional television credits include the critically acclaimed drama series *Sneaky Pete, Luck*, opposite Dustin Hoffman, and *Orphan Black*, opposite Tatiana Maslany.
>
> On the big screen, Patrick starred in the sci-fi feature film and 2019 Toronto International Film Festival selection *Clara*, the hit comedy *Old School*, directed by Todd Phillips, and 2009 Berlin Film Festival competitor *Rage*, alongside Judi Dench, Jude Law, Dianne Wiest, and Steve Buscemi. Originally from Toronto, Patrick is a graduate of the University of Southern California. He serves on the USC School of Dramatic Arts Board of Councilors and the Ojai Playwrights Conference Board of Directors.
>
> Patrick hosts the Suits Sidebar podcast with Sarah Rafferty, who played Donna on "Suits" (SuitsSidebar.com). Follow @PatrickJAdams on Instagram.

CHAPTER 2:

Visualization Is Magic

MAGIE COOK

We are so powerful. We don't even know how powerful we are. Visualization and future-casting are how all of the major goals in my life have been achieved. I didn't realize I was doing it, but, when I was younger, I would visualize myself in that moment of success, with all the exhilaration, joy, and intensity that went with it.

When I was growing up, I lived in an orphanage in Mexico, run by my parents. They always treated me and my adopted siblings poorly, because they were afraid the orphans would run away.

I used to hide out in a dark cave that I built when I was eight years old. It was in a mountaintop canyon with the drop-size of a football field. The only way to get to it was by crawling.

I wanted to become a super successful woman, so I would sit in my secret hiding place and future-cast myself into success. I imagined myself as someone with long hair (even though I have short hair now), wearing a dress and heels (which I rarely do), sitting behind a mahogany desk, even though I had never lived in or seen that kind of environment.

No matter what was going on at home, no matter how bad the poverty was, I could always visit my future self. By hoping for something better—seeing myself as happy, rather than suffering—seeing myself as already achieving those goals, opened my eyes to what's possible.

Everything that exists in this world has been a manifestation of somebody's thought. It's so easy to manifest challenges. Why not manifest success instead!

A lot of people ask me, "How did you know? How did you do it?"

I think we all have choices, and then choices become our destiny. Most of the people that I grew up with didn't make it. They ended up in cartels, in prostitution, with a drug addiction, or in prison. If you say, "I'm here and I'm suffering, and there's nothing better for me for the rest of my life," that's the direction your mindset—and your life takes.

When you commit to your dreams and wishes with laser-sharp focus, you begin to attract the people, places, and circumstances that will help you.

For eighteen years I focused on getting out. I wrote down these goals on a piece of paper, folded it up, and put it underneath my head when I slept. Then I would read my goals again when I woke up in the morning.

This is how I came to America. I was recruited to play basketball for a Mexican national team, but I broke my collarbone. A short time later, my parents took a bus tour of the United States to raise funds for their nonprofit. I was playing basketball at one of the stops in America when I got recruited. Prior to that, my dad, who was our caregiver, a doctor, told me that my dreams were over. If I had listened to him and not played that day I got recruited, I wouldn't be speaking to you today.

Hope for something better. Hold fast to your dreams and your goals. See yourself in the success you want to achieve. When we apply ourselves, in spite of our circumstances and without letting the outside world influence us, we can create magic.

> Magie Cook is the founder of Maggie's Salsa, a company that she started with just $800 and later sold to Campbell's Soup for $231 million. Growing up in poverty, Magie developed mindset strategies to help cope with the challenges; these strategies changed her life. With more than thirty years of experience, Magie helps entrepreneurs discover their hidden personal power so they can increase their revenue and make a bigger impact in the world.
>
> An internationally recognized speaker and expert in the field of business and personal development, Magie works with Fortune 100 and 500 companies, as well as A-listers, including professional athletes, influencers and thought leaders. She has been featured in publications, magazines, and on television networks such as Daystar TV, Bloomberg TV's *The American Dream*, and many more, and is the recipient of numerous awards, including the Hall of Fame at the University

of Charleston and Nobel Entrepreneur Prize in Mexico. MagieCook.com.

CHAPTER 3:

Have Purpose Behind Your Plans

JEFF BAJOREK

It's one thing to follow a process…to follow directions…to say you're going to do something and then do it. But, if you cannot connect to the bigger purpose behind what you're doing, you will never do it as well as you could.

From a sales perspective, I talk a lot about integrity and being in alignment between who you are and what you sell.

These are the five questions I ask people looking for their purpose in sales.

- Why do you believe in the company you sell for?
- Why do you believe in what you sell?
- Why do you believe in yourself?
- Why is your customer better off working with you than your competitors?
- Why do your best customers buy from you?

That last question is a trick question, because most people haven't asked it, and they need to go to their best customers and ask them. That's how you start to find your why. And if you are a solopreneur, entrepreneur, or business owner, questions like these will help you refocus and energize your business.

From a broad life perspective, if you are facing change, these questions may help you with your soul-searching in finding your purpose.

- What is really important to you?
- What do you feel passionately about?
- What are you good at?
- And how can you align those things?

Most people have a job that's really important to them, because it's how they pay their bills, how they live, how they survive. When you find something that is bigger than that or important to you, despite the fact that it's not how you make a living, that's where to start the pursuit.

For instance, if saving the penguins is important to you, think about how you can contribute to that. You can get involved from a volunteer standpoint; see if you're rewarded by the work you do in pursuit of that mission. Or you can contribute by sending a quarterly check of one hundred dollars to the Save the Penguins Foundation. That may be all you need to do to feel fulfilled, like you are making a difference. Or maybe you need to roll up your sleeves, go to Antarctica, and be part of the solution from there. Obviously, this is an extreme hypothetical, but look at your life and see how this example applies.

Following my purpose has helped me lead a much more rewarding life. I see my purpose as a leader. I lead professionally through selling. I lead as a father through sharing wisdom and setting a good example, and giving more than I receive. I lead in my marriage, my partnerships, and my friendships through giving.

When I think about my purpose as a husband, as a father, as a salesman, they're fundamentally different, but they're all inextricably linked by who I am as a person.

> Jeff Bajorek—husband, father, salesman—is host of the Rethink The Way You Sell Podcast.

CHAPTER 4:

Harness the Power of Color

HEATHER ECK

As an intuitive artist with synesthesia, my secret to success lies in understanding and working with the profound impact of color and educating people about how to intentionally create the feeling they desire through color. Color communicates profoundly, and each color resonates with a specific energy. Color is a language we all share, influencing our emotions, thoughts, and actions. When we tune in and understand how it works, it can profoundly affect our lives and well-being.

You can attract positivity, enhance productivity, and foster healing by aligning your environment, branding, and personal energy with the right colors. Colors are more than just pretty stimuli; they are powerful communicators that can shape our experiences and interactions. Think about the use of color in places that are meant to energize your spirit and make you feel young and playful—colors at theme parks and beachy boardwalks.

Red, for example, symbolizes passion and energy, making it ideal for motivating and driving action. However, too much red in a space can evoke a feeling of anger and increase blood pressure. Conversely, blue embodies calm and trust, perfect for building a serene and reliable brand image. But too much blue can make you feel down or sluggish. Yellow sparks creativity and optimism, encouraging innovative thinking. But too much yellow can make you think egotistical or overly cautious.

By intuitively and intentionally selecting and incorporating intentional colors into your home office, business, or even document designs, you can create an environment that supports your business goals and resonates with your team and audience, empowering you to take control of your surroundings and influence your experiences.

To harness this power, determine the energy you want to project and the feelings you wish to evoke. If you seek to boost creativity and innovation within your team, integrate more orange into your workspace. Wearing black to a presentation or meeting can signal an air of mystery, formality, and sophistication. Wearing red for a big presentation can signal to the audience that you're strong, powerful, and confident. Want people to immediately trust you and listen to what you say with confidence? Wear blue to your next meeting. Align your energy with colors through your clothing and workspace, and you'll notice a shift in how people respond to you and your work.

I once worked with a group to build a cohesive team spirit. Their office was predominantly gray and sterile, dampening the staff's energy and creativity. After a thorough color consultation, which involved understanding the company's goals, the team's dynamics, and the desired emotional responses, we decided to revamp the space with vibrant yellows and energizing oranges. We also introduced calming blues and calming artwork in meeting areas to promote clear and effective communication. The transformation was astounding. The team became more engaged and collaborative, and their output skyrocketed. Employees reported feeling more motivated and inspired, directly translating to better performance and business growth.

By embracing the healing and transformative power of color, you can create an environment that supports your well-being and propels your business to new heights. Whether through artwork, branding, or daily interactions, let color be your guide to success and harmony, inspiring you to reach new levels of creativity and productivity.

> Heather Eck is a multimedia abstract artist and painter who uses her gifts of clairsentience and synesthesia to interpret people, places, and experiences through color, symbol, and form. She uses her gifts to detect the most healing colors to remedy wounds, transforming vibrant energies into captivating paintings that uplift, inspire, and, ultimately, heal. HeatherEck.com.

CHAPTER 5:
Commitment Drives Everything

JEFF GOLDBERG

To be worthwhile, a goal needs to be specific: I want to be rich is too general, I want to earn $XX/year is, well, right on the money! A goal has to be exciting enough to wake you up in the morning and enough of a reach to make it worth your time and energy.

Setting goals is one thing, achieving them takes commitment.

As a coach, I always tell people I don't care what you want. I don't care what your hopes are. I don't care what your dreams are. I don't care what your wishes are as a human being. As a human being, I care about all those things, but, as your coach, the only thing I'm really interested in is what you are committed to. Because I believe commitment drives everything.

If you're not committed, then, when the going gets tough, you're going to get going, instead of actually doing what you need to do. Rarely do we find a straight path to our goal.

This is a Tony Robbins thing: you've got to attach enough pleasure to the gaining of the goal and enough pain to the lack of achievement of the goal to really drive you.

About ten years ago, an insurance a broker, who lived in Greenwich, Connecticut, had been referred to me. Steve was an ex-college football player, who was used to making $300,000 a year, and his income had plummeted. When I met Steve, he was 6'6" and weighed about four hundred pounds. A typical college athlete who'd let himself go.

His goal was to get back to $300,000 a year, so I asked him about the pleasure and pain thing. I asked, "What's the pleasure you're going to reward yourself with when you achieve this goal?" And Steve said, "Because my income has been going down the last few years, I haven't really been able to take my family on a nice vacation. So, I'm going to take them on the best vacation to St. Lucia that they've ever been on in their entire lives."

Then I said, "Let's talk about pain. On the off-chance that we can't achieve this goal, what are you going to do?"

He thought about it for a couple of moments, and said, "I will walk around my block in January." (Note: This is not like in New York City, where you walk around a block in five minutes; the blocks in Greenwich could be a mile.) Now, this is a guy who doesn't like exercise, so I said, "Not bad. Can we make it more painful?"

"How about if I walk around the block twice in January," was his counteroffer.

After a bit more back-and-forth, I got him to agree that, if he did not achieve his goal of $300,000, he would walk around his block in January in a bikini and high heels with me walking behind him and videotaping him the whole time.

Needless to say, I do not have that videotape. He achieved his goal!

Attaching enough pain or enough pleasure to an outcome really helps you stay motivated to achieve your goals. Almost anything is possible with commitment.

> Jeff Goldberg is a sales coach and trainer, and president of JG&A. Through training, coaching, mentoring, and managing, he's helped tens of thousands of salespeople internationally achieve sustainable sales increases. He's also a stand-up comedian and co-author of *How to Be Your Own Coach* and *Leverage Your Laziness!* JGSalesPro.com.

CHAPTER 6:

Endurance and Perseverance

CHRISTINE TOY JOHNSON

It's easy to get clouded by images of what we think success should look like. The truth is success is different for everyone. Everybody has different kinds of goals, within both their career and personal life. We need to believe we will achieve them!

I'm an actor, writer, director, and advocate for inclusion. In a career that's impossible at best and full of challenges and rejection, it's easy to go down a rabbit hole of sadness and despair, at all points on your journey. The reality is, I am still here. I've been working professionally as an actor for my entire adult life and as a writer for the last twenty or so years.

The key to endurance is gratitude, inspiration, and reinvention.

Gratitude. Be thankful for the good in your life—opportunities and people—and celebrate all of your accomplishments, big and small. In many creative fields, and in fields like entrepreneurship, where you are driven by a passion to do something, it is not necessarily for financial gain. If you do achieve financial gain, great. But that's not the engine that keeps you going. I often think about how grateful I am for my life in the theatre: that I get to express myself, my hopes, my dreams, the world as I'd like to see it, through various ways of storytelling. What a gift! Remembering this keeps me centered and gets me through the rough patches.

Inspiration. Stay inspired by what you've achieved up to that moment and keep building on it. Look at things from a place of abundance, not lack. The inner dialogue is not, "I *need* to do this, because I don't have that." It should be, "I *want* to do this, because I have the potential to do more."

As a writer, I send out scripts, or enter fellowships, competitions, or whatever, and I often get rejections. That's just the way it is. It's a numbers game: there's a lot of a lot of content out there; people are looking for different things.

I often find, when I feel like I should just throw that script in the garbage or press delete, invariably I bounce back like I'm on a trampoline. My inner voice says, "Oh, wait! I have an idea for a new project." I can't even give you one example of that; it happens all the time. Now I know, when I get really sad or dejected, I try not to worry, because a new idea is on its way. Maybe the experience of having that happen so many times gives me some kind of comfort and reassurance.

Reinvention. Here's what's different about being an actor and being a writer on a very fundamental level. As an actor, you are an interpretive artist; as a writer, you are a generative artist. For a lot of actors of color like me, the reason we started writing is because we didn't see the opportunities for people who looked like us. Stop waiting. You don't need permission. Keep working on your next great idea. And start over as many times as you want. There's no expiration date on your creativity.

Also: It's really important to create practical strategies, as well as fantastical strategies, as you move forward on your goal journey. My husband has actually helped me see this a lot. I will think very practically: How can I do this in a short, quick, not-very-expensive way? Or how can I achieve something grassroots? I'm going to get my hands dirty, but that's okay. He always encourages me to think even bigger. What that does is, it helps you expand your imagination. And who knows what will come from that? I think that taking those risks can be scary, but it's also so worth it.

Success is not always what you imagine it should look like. Sometimes it's even better.

> Christine Toy Johnson is a Tony- and Obie-honored, multiple-award-winning writer, actor, and advocate for inclusion. As an actor, she's been featured on Broadway, off-Broadway, national tours, regionally, in film, and on TV. Highlights include Season 2 of Marvel's *Iron Fist*, the first national tour of *Come From Away*, and various shows at the Guthrie, Williamstown, and the Public. Her written works have been produced and/or developed by the Roundabout, O'Neill, Abingdon, Ars Nova, Florida Studio Theatre, Prospect Theatre, Weston Playhouse, Village Theatre, Goodspeed Opera House, etc., and are included in the Library of Congress's Asian Pacific

American Playwrights Collection. Christine is treasurer of the Dramatists Guild, founder of the Asian American Theatre Artists Collective, co-founder of AAPAC. Alum of BMI, The Writers Lab, and Sarah Lawrence College. Details at ChristineToyJohnson.com.

CHAPTER 7:

Follow the Five Ps

WENDY DIAMOND

My number one tip for success is to have purpose, passion, persistence, perseverance, and puppy love! Stay focused on your purpose, let your passion drive you, keep going even when things get tough with persistence, and never give up with perseverance. And adopt a dog, so you have lots of puppy love when times get ruff!

Purpose: As an entrepreneur, it's not easy, but when you have a mission as significant as making a difference in the world, it gives you the strength to fight for it. When your purpose is clear, you're more willing to overcome obstacles to make it happen.

Passion: You need to be so passionate that everyone around you knows what you're doing. Your passion should be so strong that it convinces you there is nothing that can stand in your way.

Persistence: Personally, I've received what feels like a million nos, but those few yeses have helped me create the impact

I have today. It's the persistence to keep going, even after countless rejections, that eventually leads to success.

Perseverance: Never give up! Pivot if you need to, but don't give up on your dreams. The greatest gift of hard work is knowing that you can make it happen. Working hard doesn't mean just a day or a month; it may take twenty years. Enjoy the journey, and you'll never regret what you didn't do!

Puppy Love: Always have a pup or pet by your side. There's no better unconditional love, especially when you're on the entrepreneurial roller coaster. The innocence of this love has been proven to help people mentally and emotionally. Having a furry friend can provide the comfort and joy you need to keep going.

With these five Ps, you'll be well on your way to achieving your dreams!

I founded Animal Fair Media, Inc., the premiere pet lifestyle media company, in 1999. After adopting a purebred Maltese, Lucky Diamond, and Russian blue cat, Pasha Diamond, from the city shelter, and learning that twelve million animals were euthanized each year, I set out to inspire and educate the world.

At that time, pets were rarely featured in media, celebrities weren't seen with pets, and there was little integration of pets into pop culture. I knew that, by showing people they could adopt any breed, size, age, or color of pet, we could encourage people to adopt versus buy! So, I brought celebrities and pop culture into the world of animal rescue and welfare, coining the term "pet lifestyle, yappy hour." Now, the number of animals euthanized annually has dropped to less than two million, and pets are everywhere in media.

It's gratifying to see how integrating pets into mainstream culture has made such a positive impact on animal welfare. Very few people know that, for the first three years, I worked tirelessly, often putting in twenty-four-hour days, without making any money. Even Purina initially declined to support us because we pioneered the premier pet fashion show, featuring rescue dogs dressed by famous fashion designers to raise awareness and funds for animal rescue. It's ironic that they now sponsor one of the largest pet fashion shows.

> Wendy Diamond is an internationally renowned impact entrepreneur, impact investor, animal advocate, humanitarian, bestselling author, TV personality, and DO GOODer! She is the founder of Animal Fair Media, Inc. (AnimalFair.com), founder of LDP Ventures (SFO), which invests in social impact disruptive technologies, and CEO/founder of the Women's Entrepreneurship Day Organization. WEDO, #ChooseWOMEN, is a nongovernmental philanthropic volunteer organization on a global mission influencing policy-making, and stimulating economic advancement, with a special focus on eradicating poverty, making a positive impact, and creating a brighter future for women entrepreneurs worldwide!
>
> Wendy has authored ten widely celebrated books, garnered three Guinness World Records, and has been a featured keynote speaker at the United Nations, World Economic Forum, and Harvard University.

CHAPTER 8:

Preserve Time to Nurture Your Business

JESS DEWELL

When you take the time to understand the priorities of your business, you are able to assess which opportunities will advance you to your goals.

Each week, I do something I call a Present Retreat™. I go into my office, close the door, and turn off notifications on all of my devices. It is protected time, which can be a little bit of a respite in addition to being action-oriented, so that the deep work can happen.

I began this practice several years ago because I was feeling overwhelmed. It felt like every day, minute to minute, priorities were changing. I wasn't considering how my decisions would affect me in three to five years, because the only things on my mind were putting out fires and getting through the next five minutes. It turns out, there's actually a cost to mentally switching gears all the time. Your business suffers, and your body goes into burnout mode.

I decided there's got to be a better way.

I started doing Present Retreats in two-hour blocks of time on Mondays; now my entire Monday is reserved for this work.

I ask myself questions, like:

- How is my business performing?
- Are we on task for the priorities that we have set?
- What are the new opportunities that have come in?
- Is there anything I need to reprioritize?

Those buckets enable me to assess my business while planning for the future. As a bonus, it saves a lot of time. I actually work a little less the rest of the week.

When someone approaches me with an opportunity, I know what's going to be a no right off the bat. (It's almost ten nos to every yes.) If an opportunity comes in on a Tuesday, and it's not a no, I hit the pause button and respond after my next Monday session. I want to be able to evaluate the possible yeses with a clear mind.

One of my clients was in complete and utter burnout mode, and came back from her first Present Retreat really excited about her business. She'd forgotten how much fun her business actually was. It was right there in front of her, but she lost sight of it. She was stuck in the weeds and never had a chance to see how much her business was producing on all levels: revenue and profit, as well as contribution to the community.

Another client thought they were an amazing, awesome leader, which was not the most accurate assessment at the time. Through this work, they found ways to improve their communication with their team, delegate, and set up the business up for success.

A third client used this process to double their revenues, without increasing the number of employees. They were in a better position to evaluate the projects that came in and said yes to more of the right projects.

Saying yes to things that are out of alignment—taking action on things that should be nos—is the quickest way to stop making progress.

The *best* way to keep making progress is consistently giving yourself the time to figure out, prioritize, and move forward on your business initiatives.

> Jess Dewell is Founder and CEO of Red Direction and brings more than twenty years of advising, consulting, and facilitation experience in operational strategy and organizational culture, where values and purpose intersect. Both practical and unexpected, her views tune into the uniqueness of any organization. Jess is also the host of the *Bold Business Podcast*. Learn more at RedDirection.com.

BONUS CHAPTER:
Use Your Superpowers to Create a Life Full of Impact

ALEX AMOUYEL

We all want to do good in the world, and live a life full of impact, purpose, and meaning. Too often, though, we do not know where to start. I am here to tell you that you can start right now, and that we need everyone to get involved if we are going to solve the world's greatest challenges.

The first step is to think about your own superpowers: What makes you unique? What are you particularly good at? What gives you the most energy? Once you have that, you can think about the problems that need to be solved, whether that is in your community, your city, your country, or the world. Rather than "finding a passion," find a problem you want to punch, one that keeps you up at night, and/or one that deeply resonates with you in some way.

At the intersection of your superpowers and a real problem, affecting millions or billions of people, lies your purpose. Congrats! You're halfway there! This does not mean you should quit your day job. Many people may not be able to do that right away. The next step is to move toward directing 10 percent of your time and money toward your purpose. Then you can make a plan to move closer and closer toward living a life full of impact.

In my early twenties, I did a master's in international relations and specialized in human rights and security. My dream was to work for an organization such as Human Rights Watch or Save the Children. I applied to both of these organizations; they had fellowships which paid very little, but I was okay with that. I never even got an interview for them and was devastated at the time.

Unsure of my next steps, I applied to a number of strategy consulting firms, as many of my peers were doing. I ended up getting three job offers and took a position with the Boston Consulting Group (BCG) in London. I did this partly because they boasted of the pro-bono partnerships they had with the World Food Programme and Save the Children itself.

Fast-forward eighteen months at BCG, after a string of pharma and private equity clients. I managed to get staffed on a four-month pro-bono Save the Children project with BCG. It was one of my dream organizations, and I loved every minute of it! And, when that team had a full-time role open up a few months after that, I jumped at the opportunity. That role kick-started the rest of my career in the social impact space.

Why am I telling you this? The team I joined at Save the Children was called Unified Presence. It was all ex-consultants and ex-accountants because the team was all about creating joint ventures and merging existing Save the Children entities. Prior to my arrival, Save the Children had nine offices operating in Ethiopia, five in Kenya, and many more across the world. You see, Save the Children had developed initially as a franchise of independent members, which is great for growing quickly and when your money is tied to specific fundraising countries. However, that made no sense in the countries where they currently had programs. It also made little sense to donors as they grew, especially when several Europe-based Save the Children members would apply and thus compete for the same European Union funding! To be clear, many big NGOs, including Doctors Without Borders, Action Against Hunger, Oxfam, and Plan International, were or are still set up that way.

The team I joined was all about unifying Save the Children's work, ultimately creating one Save the Children International programming headquarters in London. This included harmonizing all the processes and systems that went with this.

I could never have been on that team without the experience I had acquired as a strategy consultant at BCG. It was a unique skillset and experience that very few people at Save the Children had. That was thus my superpower, and what I could bring to the table to make everyone else's work better and more impactful!

Alex Amouyel is the president and CEO of Newman's Own Foundation and the author of *The Answer is You: A Guidebook to Creating a Life Full of Impact*. Get in touch or follow her on LinkedIn.

PART 2 –
WELL-BEING

Tune into what works best for you and your body, and you will operate at the top of your game.

CHAPTER 9:

Seek Harmony, Not Balance

ELAINE HALL

My personal mission is to bring out the best in myself and others with a vision to change the way the world perceives neurodivergence and disability. As a social introvert, and being neurodivergent myself, my time to myself is precious. From this point of centeredness, I can create new ideas, feel energized to collaborate on projects with others, and at the same time, be conscious of not overextending myself.

Self-care in the morning is a priority. I am a very early riser; five in the morning is my favorite time of day. (I will often take a twenty- to thirty-minute nap around three in the afternoon, especially when I need to be out in the evening.) I begin each day with a yoga stretch, meditation, and personal writing.

By centering myself first, I can draw upon the wisdom of the universe. I listen to inspiring speakers, such as Marci Shimoff, Dr. Sue Morter, and others to bring in a spiritual component to incorporate throughout my day.

I try to schedule all meetings after 11:30 a.m., so I can have my mornings for my own personal reflection, deep work, and important projects. An evening walk with my husband or a friend brings the day to a beautiful close. Before I go to bed, I look over my schedule/plans for the next day. I keep a pad of paper by my bedside in case any ideas come up before I go to sleep—and if/when I wake up in the middle of the night with an idea or a "to-do" I forgot about.

One more thing: I stop work every Friday before sundown and do not work again until Monday at 11:00 a.m. I will not look over emails until Sunday, even during a busy time. And if I have a pressing project, I will work a bit on Sunday—but, as a rule, I take the weekends off.

My positive relationships with my husband and my adult son (who is nonspeaking and neurodivergent) are essential. And I plan accordingly to prioritize time with them. Rather than trying to achieve "balance," I seek "harmony."

One of my greatest challenges is also one of my greatest blessings. I receive an abundance of work opportunities, involving coaching, consulting, speaking, being on TV and film sets to ensure access, etc. It is essential for me to create my own mission statement and stay focused on personal projects, lest I get tossed and turned into advocating for others and putting my own projects aside.

Elaine Hall, founder of The Miracle Project (TheMiracleProject.org), and star of the HBO Emmy-winning film *Autism: The Musical*, is an international speaker, author, media personality, consultant, and access coordinator for TV, film, and theatre. Her memoir, *Now I See the Moon*, was selected by the United Nations for World Autism Awareness Day. She has been featured on CNN, OWN, CBS, in the *NYT*, *WSJ*, and *Boston Globe*, among others, for her innovative contributions to the autistic, neurodivergent, and entertainment communities. Elaine-Hall.com.

CHAPTER 10:

Stand Up! It's Harder Than It Sounds

CHRIS LEVINSON

When we're laser-focused on the task at hand—everything from hitting a deadline to finishing the grocery list—we have a tendency to clench. Jaw locked, shoulders hunched, shallow breathing. Basically, we assume the fetal position, though sitting up. It becomes all about crossing the finish line, and we're only going to get there hunched over in a fever dream. Not so much.

If we power through with blinders on, not to mention only sipping air rather than actually breathing, it shows in the work. I know, I know. What you're doing can't wait. You have limited time, with only so much focus and energy to spare. Reading this, every fiber of your being is saying, "Are you nuts? No! I can't possibly make time for that!" But amazing things happen when you do. Just try it. Stand up.

And here's where I admit that's a bit of a cheat. Because, by standing up, you're doing so much more. You're breaking the spell. No joke. The minute your spine straightens and a full breath of actual air fills your lungs, your brain clears. And standing up often leads to movement. It can be around the kitchen or office, all the way to (gasp!) outside. And trust me, things get clearer. The weight of everything feels a tad lighter, more manageable. Ideas come that wouldn't have, if you'd stayed locked to your computer screen. Try it. I dare you.

I pitched and sold a television pilot. That means I had dreamed up a world, every character who inhabited it, their backstories, and where they'd go over the course of a first season. My genre is crime/thrillers, so my plots tend to be tight and twisty. And this one just wasn't working. This is not something I was ready to tell the streamer who was paying me to write it.

There I was, hunched over my computer in the dim light of my office, sipping air... And then I stood up. I have no idea what inspired it. Possibly the voice of my mom—always wise—or was it the lack of blood flow to my lower extremities? Whatever the cause, I stood up. And once I was up, I moved around my office a bit. And then, yep, I went outside. I stood in my backyard, looked up at the sky, and the insanity in my head quieted down a bit.

I'm not saying it went away and all the problems of the world were solved. But a plot point that had been holding me up, a way to bridge two timelines that just wasn't clicking while I was lock-jawed in my desk chair, fell into place. It had been there all along. I just needed to stand up to let it out.

CHAPTER 10: STAND UP! IT'S HARDER THAN IT SOUNDS

> Chris Levinson is a writer, creator, and executive producer, who cut her teeth on such iconic shows as *Party of Five*, *Dawson's Creek*, and *Charmed*. Her love of crime drama brought her to *Law & Order*, where she penned an Emmy-nominated episode. She has shot three original pilots and sold projects to FX, Hulu, Peacock, Paramount+, NBC, USA, Amazon, and FOX.
>
> Chris has worked with the CIA and the New America Foundation in establishing ties between showrunners and the agency's cyber security experts. She is a nonresident fellow with CSIS in their Smart Women, Smart Power initiative, working specifically with NATO on their global story. Chris studied English at Stanford and at St. Catherine's College, University of Oxford. Find Chris on IMDB.com.

CHAPTER 11:

Listen to Your Body. Your Body Knows Everything.

MICHAEL LENNOX

One of the ways I have found success is that I've allowed my body to find its natural rhythm. When I focus on my body's movement, then it gets done what it needs to get done, and my capacity for productivity increases.

How I started living in my body at age forty is radically different than the first forty years. I found that, when my body *works with* time, it transcends the old paradigm of *managing* time (forcing your body to do things) to get your goals accomplished.

In 2003, 2004, when I was thirty-nine, forty years old, I no longer had to show up to a corporate job; I was doing my doctoral dissertation. I was very active, but organically, I found myself wanting to get up earlier and go to sleep earlier. I found that interesting, and I noticed that change.

Then something interesting happened in 2005, when I needed to be supported. Somebody brought me into his home for nine years, while I finished my doctorate, did my dissertation, got the research published, and wrote my first book. I was living in his house, and I hated interacting with my "roommate" so much that I forced myself to stay in bed till 8:15 a.m., after he left for work. I got used to that schedule, but it didn't do me any favors.

When I moved out on my own in 2013, I found there was nothing stopping me from returning to that organic rhythm. It was almost instantaneous that my body wanted to start before the sun rose, and that the moment the sun went down at four or five o'clock, I was done.

- I have this wave of energy at like five, six, seven, eight a.m.
- I have a shift drop at nine a.m. until about ten or eleven a.m. It's a horrible time for me. It's when I'm sad and uncomfortable and anxious, though each day to a different extent.
- And then I get this sweet spot again at eleven a.m. That's why I do all of my first clients or interviews, anything I have to schedule with anyone, at that time.

When I am drawn to collaborate with someone, I've found that it needs to work with my clock. It's like how, if I were drawn to dating a night owl, I'd be like, "You're hot, but I ain't staying up."

I know intimately how my circadian rhythms move every day, as a consistent patterning, not an idea. This works because I know who I am, I know how I serve, and I love my work. That was already in place once I finally had the freedom to live any way that my body wanted.

Once I started operating like this, my productivity of the last ten years outweighed anything for the first fifty.

> Dr. Michael Lennox is a psychologist, astrologer, and expert in dreams and dream interpretation. He has appeared on SyFy, MTV, NBC, and countless radio shows and podcasts. Dr. Lennox leads workshops and retreats all over the United States, conducts a worldwide private practice based in Southern California, and can be found sharing his knowledge on social media and through his weekly podcast, Conscious Embodiment: Astrology and Dreams with Dr. Michael Lennox. He is also the author of *Psychic Dreamer*, *Llewellyn's Complete Dictionary of Dreams*, *Llewellyn's Little Book of Dreams*, and *Dream Sight*. Visit him at MichaelLennox.com.

CHAPTER 12:

Energy Management

MARI SMITH

Energy management is not just about stamina; it's managing your brain capacity and interactions with others. Whether you are a solo business owner with a small team—like I am—an entrepreneur, a consultant, or a creative, it's important to be focused on your health and well-being. This covers the gamut from sleep to nutrition to self-care.

I've been studying the Human Design System for four years, and I just love it. It is holistically based and has provided me with profound insights into my own self, based on my date, time, and place of birth. It's a fusion of astrology, the I Ching, quantum physics, genetics, biology, and more. It is the most accurate system I've ever come across, and I've reviewed practically all of them.

Through my studies of Human Design, I have much more compassion for myself. One of my genetic propensities is called "Extremes," so I need to be mindful of taking breaks, as I can overdo things. I also know that rushing and pushing and setting hard deadlines is not healthy for my body. I need a lot of spaciousness to complete projects and drive to destinations, for example.

Obviously, you have to produce things in the workplace. So, at some point, there's going to be a deadline. I try to allow myself plenty of time to get things done. I've gotten a lot better, but sometimes, when I feel a bit overscheduled, I'll just trust my gut when I need to make a change. For instance, I'll ask a client, "Would you be okay if we moved your appointment to next week?" And they're like, "Oh, thank goodness, I had something come up anyway, and I really wanted to move it." I love how this adjustment often works out for everyone's benefit.

I'm also tuned in to my energy when speaking at conferences and other events. I don't travel as much as I did a few years ago, but I am still a regular speaker at certain events.

Knowing my own self so deeply now, I realize I have a very sensitive body type. I'm sensitive to EMF (electromagnetic fields), frequencies, sounds, and smells. I also know that I digest food better in an environment with no or low sound. Therefore, going out to dinners in raucous, loud restaurants, or attending mixers in noisy bars really impacts me, especially as a public speaker. I can't project my voice very well in those environments. So, I'll pop in for twenty minutes or so to say a quick hello. Then I will retreat to my hotel, get room service, eat alone peacefully, and prepare for my talk.

When I've got a speaking engagement, I will do everything I can to build up reserves of energy. That means getting plenty of sleep and watching what I eat the night before. My sensitive body doesn't tolerate alcohol these days, and I don't do coffee, either.

So, when it's time to present on stage, I can really put a lot of energy out there. And I often happily take questions from audience members long after I'm off the stage. If there's a line or group of people who want to talk to me, I'll still be talking to them as much as two hours later. I'll be the last one to leave the building. Then I'll go crash in my room by myself and replenish, especially if I am back the next day.

When you understand at a deep level how your own, unique body functions and you manage your energy at the most optimal level, you'll show up as your best self in work and in life. You'll be more present and make more authentic connections. And your brain will operate more optimally, so you can learn better and do your best work for your clients.

> Often referred to as "the Queen of Facebook," Mari Smith is widely known as the premier Facebook marketing expert and a top social media thought leader. *Forbes* describes Mari as "the preeminent Facebook expert. Even Facebook asks for her help." IBM named Mari one of seven women who are shaping digital marketing. She is an in-demand keynote speaker, dynamic live webinar host, savvy corporate social media strategist and trainer, and popular brand ambassador. She is the author of *The New Relationship Marketing* and co-author of *Facebook Marketing: An Hour a Day*. And Mari now integrates aspects of the Human Design system into her social media marketing courses to help entrepreneurs and SMBs

grow their businesses in a much more authentic, impactful, and successful way. MariSmith.com.

CHAPTER 13:

Be Honest with Yourself

ANGELA MILLER BARTON

When embarking on initiatives, personal and professional—and, even more importantly, when resisting them—it's really important to be honest with yourself.

Ask yourself:

- Do I want to do this goal?
- Do I want to achieve this goal?
- Or do I just want the feeling that I think achieving this goal will get me?

As a personal trainer, yoga teacher, and coach, people tell me all the time what they think they should be working on. For instance, "I should probably quit smoking," or, "I probably should lose weight."

Better that they should be honest with themselves, and ask, "Am I ready to let go of the smoking or my pint-of-ice-cream-a-night habit?" And, if I'm not ready, "What am I willing to do?"

While some of the things we do (habits) may not be good for us, there's usually a very good reason for them. Granted, quitting smoking may be a little tougher than resisting the need for ice cream. Yet, when you address the underlying cause—perhaps stress is the problem that's causing you to smoke or overindulge—you will more likely be able to resolve what has you conflicted.

For example, in fall 2023, I was supposed to run a hundred-mile race. It was a difficult year for me; I'd had two deaths in the family and it had hit me really hard. I was not in an emotional, mental, or physical state to start training.

Preparing for a race is a big undertaking, kind of like writing a book or looking for a new job. I realized I didn't have the capacity to put what was necessary into it. I had to be honest with myself. Not only did I not think I could do it, I wasn't even sure I wanted to do it. And that took a little bit of courage—it was a real ego-bruiser—to bail on something I'd previously committed to do.

When I finally said the words out loud—when I told my husband, "I just can't do it"—his reaction was simply, "Okay." He didn't care. Nobody else that I told cared. I would have pushed myself to do something I had no business doing at that particular time, all because I thought other people might be disappointed in me.

Being honest with myself enabled me to get a little more sleep, not exercise to the extreme, and slowly recover from my personal losses. I was still mourning, and I really needed that time.

Five months later, I *was* ready. I ran a race, and it was a wonderful experience. It was good for me, and I had a great time!

Being honest doesn't mean, "Not ever." Sometimes it just means, "Not right now."

> Angela Miller Barton is a personal trainer, yoga instructor, and program coordinator for Wellcoaches membership. Learn more at Wellcoaches.com.

CHAPTER 14:

Think Positively and Believe in Yourself

JENNIFER WATSON

Mindset is everything. So many people get overwhelmed with their projects, dreams, and goals. If you wait for perfection—that right moment—it will never happen. Life is messy. Take a deep breath, make a plan, set goals, take action, and believe in the most positive outcome!

Sometimes in your journey, you may make a wrong turn or trust someone who breaks your heart. If that happens, give yourself a moment, dust yourself off, and keep moving toward your goals. Stay focused and positive, so you always have your dreams in sight. Remember, no matter the circumstance, there's always something positive you can learn and take from the experience, even if it's a little hard to find at first.

Visualization is a tool I use every single day. I started doing it even before I realized I was! Growing up, I was a competitive gymnast. Before I did my routines, especially on balance beam, I would close my eyes and visualize the entire routine in my head. I would go through every skill, sticking everything, including my landing. Then I would open my eyes and nail my routine, just as I'd imagined it!

As an adult, a single mom, an entrepreneur, a meteorologist, and a storm chaser, this is a skill I still use.

Every day, before I get out of bed, I close my eyes and envision how I want each part of my day to go. This includes work meetings, errands, on-air broadcasts, you name it! I also go through the emotions, the excitement of how I'm going to feel after accomplishing every task. Then I get out of bed and make it happen. With visualization and a positive attitude, there isn't anything you can't do. I believe in your power, your strength, your brilliance. So go out there and be the best *you* that you can be!

Jennifer Watson is an Emmy-winning TV personality, global marketing and social media strategist, meteorologist on the Weather Channel, speaker, and podcaster. Jennifer is a dynamic talent with a passion for every aspect of digital media, from building brand strategies and creating content plans to getting executive buy-in. She motivates audiences from the stage and drives engagement, including launching numerous Facebook Live campaigns for the biggest weather brand, garnering millions of views. She has been featured in *Chief Content Marketer Magazine* and on stage at Content Marketing World, Social Fresh, Social Media Marketing World, and Social Shake-Up, to name a few. Her podcast can be found at StormFrontFreaks.com. Follow @JenniferWeather on Instagram/TikTok.

CHAPTER 15:

Remove the Roadblocks

AMY FERRIS

I've always believed that, with any goal, if it's possible, it's not big enough. Each one of us has the ability and the capability to achieve whatever we set our minds to. And no one—not even ourselves—has the ability to take that away from us.

If we can't do something, it's mostly because we haven't done it before. Maybe we tried and we didn't succeed. Chances are, what stops us isn't a roadblock that's in front of us, it's a roadblock that's inside of us.

We need to put more faith in our own lives and stop listening to all those old tapes that keep repeating themselves. Every time you hear in your head, "You can't do that" or "You're not good enough," tell that voice to "Stop!" Put it in the recycling bin and have it come out as something that's much more durable and useful for your own life.

Everyone has incredible insecurities. It's not like they magically go away or dissolve. But we can reframe them. Some people get up on a stage and share this really cool, empowering message. Then, when they get off the stage, and you talk to them, you realize they're as vulnerable and insecure as the rest of us. The difference is that they took what they have been through and learned how to transform it into something that works for them, rather than against them.

Whenever I've gotten a rejection letter—I submitted a book proposal or whatever, and got a letter saying, "No, thank you"—I used to go, "Oh, no. That person doesn't like it." Now I think, "Okay. That person read it. It's not their thing. Let me find somebody who gets me, who connects with this."

We put so much value in other people's opinion of us. We forget that our opinion of our own life and our own work is what really matters.

When we set out to create stuff, thinking, "Will they like it?" we're setting ourselves up for not being liked, for failure, for rejection. If we write, paint, or create something because we want to, because it's important to us, because it makes us happy, now we're getting somewhere. That kind of mindset keeps us from being disappointed and frees us from being scared of rejection.

Not everyone is going to like what we do. But what's really important is when people have a real reaction. And even if they don't like what we've written, we should really applaud ourselves, because we've had an effect on them.

The overall message is: "You matter!"

One thing that I would add—and it's something that I try really hard to live by and apply to my own daily life—is that, if you're looking to be validated by the outside world, you will never feel satisfied.

It's great when people love what we do. It's wonderful when we get kudos. But if we're looking for other people to keep our heart pumping, that's hard. We have to really fall in love with our own lives, with what we do, and with the entire journey. I wholeheartedly believe that we owe it to ourselves to see our dreams come to fruition, and not let anyone stop us…and that includes us.

> Amy Ferris is an author, screenwriter, editor, and playwright. Her latest is *Mighty Gorgeous: A Little Book About Messy Love* (SheWrites Press, 2023). Her memoir, *Marrying George Clooney: Confessions From A Midlife Crisis* (Seal Press), debuted theatrically (Off-Broadway @ CAP 21 Theatre) in 2012. Ruth Pennebaker of the *New York Times* called her memoir "poignant, free-wheeling, cranky and funny." Amy edited the anthology *Shades of Blue, Writers on Depression, Suicide and Feeling Blue* (Seal Press), co-edited the anthology *Dancing at the Shame Prom* (Seal Press), and has contributed to numerous anthologies. She has written for both film and TV. Her screenplays include *Mr. Wonderful* (directed by Anthony Minghella) and *Funny Valentines* (directed by Julie Dash). She co-authored *Old School Love* (HarperCollins, 2021) with Rev. Run of Run-DMC fame.
>
> Amy was honored as one of Twenty-One Leaders for the Twenty-First Century by Women's eNews, and named one of "Twelve Women Who Changed the World" in 2021 by NextTribe. Amy is a co-founder of the Milford Readers and Writers Festival. Follow Amy: Facebook.com/amy.ferris.

BONUS CHAPTER:

Worrying Is a Waste of Time

JEFF PULVER

Worry paralyzes you. It's unnerving. It prohibits you from being your best self. Let go of worry, and you release what you cannot control. When you focus on what you can control, you will find success.

Whenever I am faced with an opportunity or challenge, I imagine myself getting through the moment. I give myself a chance to breathe, feel, and unlock whatever blockages I am facing. Then I can face the situation from a position of power.

To manifest your power:

Set Clear Intentions: Be specific about what you want. Define success in clear, concrete terms. For example, instead of saying, "I want my business to be successful," specify, "I want my business to reach $1 million in revenue by the end of the year."

Visualize Your Desired Outcome: Spend time each day visualizing your goal as if it's already achieved. See it, feel it, and experience it in your mind as vividly as possible.

Speak It Out Loud: The power of verbal affirmations. Speak your intentions out loud with conviction.

Write It Down: Put your goals and vision in writing. This helps to crystallize your thoughts and makes your intentions feel more real and tangible.

Share It with Others: Tell someone you trust about your vision. This creates a sense of accountability and makes your goal feel more real.

Feel Worthy of Receiving: Allow yourself to feel that you are good enough and worthy enough to receive what you're asking for. Many people block their own manifestations because, deep down, they don't feel deserving of success.

Feel the Emotions of Achievement: With your eyes still closed, let yourself feel the emotions you would experience if you had already achieved your goal. Feel the joy, the excitement, and the sense of accomplishment. These emotions are powerful attractors.

When I brought back my VON conferences, at first, it was just an idea. Then I imagined it could be successful. I set things in motion, and it turned into reality less than four months later.

My dad spent most of my life telling me and my sisters that worrying is a waste of time. It wasn't until I was writing his eulogy, thinking back on our time together, that the truth of his philosophy really hit me.

> Jeff Pulver is an American internet entrepreneur and futurist known for his work as an innovator in the field of voice over internet protocol (VoIP). He has been a pioneer in the communications industry, founding several influential organizations and events, including the VON conferences, and advocating for the future of internet-based communications. Pulver.com.

PART 3 -

ACTION

Embrace who you are; proceed with integrity.

CHAPTER 16:

It Always Pays to Reach

ARTHUR SMITH

My philosophy is that we make our own good fortune. The message at the heart of my memoir, *REACH: Hard Lessons and Learned Truths from a Lifetime in Television*, is that, in life and in business, it always pays to reach. I've never been one of those people who waits for the next opportunity to present itself on its own. I'm always out there looking for it, reaching for it, doing everything I can to make it a part of my reality. Ultimately, one reach will lead to another.

When you spend a lifetime reaching, you become wired to think of what lies ahead. You meet a goal and start in right away on the next goal. Naturally, reaching alone doesn't always get it done. It is not enough to simply set your sights on a goal. You have to earn your way to it. Sometimes there's a hurdle you can't seem to get past or maybe it's just an opportunity that doesn't have your name on it. Even when you're on a roll, you'll occasionally need to slow that roll to match your reality. Most often, you'll need a measure of persistence to help you along. And sometimes, you'll need to play the long game and wait for the marketplace and the moment to align with your vision.

In my career, I came to see disappointments as learning experiences, and I have also realized that in almost every case, everything was meant to be. Everyone at some point will experience setbacks, and it is how one picks themselves up from those moments where success is found.

Reaching toward goal after goal has propelled me into working with some of the most iconic and interesting people in the world and founding an award-winning production company, which has produced over two hundred shows. As I look at my lifetime in television, I know for sure that none of this would have been achieved had I not had the audacity and the confidence to reach again and again.

Growth—big or small—personal or professional—is essential to one's happiness. Sometimes growth just happens on its own. But then there are other times, like when you're reaching, when you're able to take matters into your own hands and achieve greater growth and greater success on an accelerated timetable.

After I became the youngest-ever head of CBC Sports in Canada, it came time to consider some kind of next career move. This was the reach that propelled my biggest life change into motion when I moved to the United States, by invitation of one of the most famous producers in the world at the time, Dick Clark.

My reach was a letter. A letter to him that I would never have written if some of my other reaches hadn't been so quick to write me off. In it, I shared my story of how I wanted to be back in the trenches developing and producing entertainment programming, a genre his company was the leader in. I took a risk and closed the letter with the following bold strokes: "Thank you for taking the time to read this letter because I can appreciate how busy you are, but reading this letter is not a waste of your time and meeting me will not be either."

A week later, I received an invitation to Los Angeles for an interview with the one and only Dick Clark. I came prepared with a bunch of ideas. I was good and ready. We got right into it, going through every single one of those ideas. Right away, it felt to me like we had an easy professional rapport, almost like we were already working together. Sure enough, three weeks later to the day, Dick called and offered me a job. He moved me to Los Angeles, became a huge mentor, and helped set my life on a whole new course in one of the luckiest breaks of my career.

Ultimately, I think what we can take away from my personal story about reaching is, if you let fear be your guide, you will most likely be stuck in neutral. If you're not sure what you want or what you want to do, take your best guess. Once you start moving in a direction, even if it's the wrong one, you will learn what you don't like. Be prepared to stumble into a new job, or a new field, or a new project you never thought you would like. It's important to get going, get moving, even. Life is a series of experiments. Some of them are field experiments, but we can learn from them anyway. Accept the fact that, if you're reaching, you're going to be at least a little bit vulnerable. Being dedicated, working hard, and having a positive attitude will make you less vulnerable.

Failure is not the end of the road, it's a detour or redirect. As you look ahead, visualize where you want to go. The mind, as we all know, is a powerful tool. You'll be surprised by how comfortable you will be when you get there if you have spent quality time visualizing it.

Good luck, fellow reachers!

> Arthur Smith has been a hands-on, trendsetting producer in the unscripted television space, creating innovative, larger-than-life formats as the founder and CEO of A. Smith & Co. Productions for over two decades and counting. His memoir, *REACH: Hard Lessons and Learned Truths from a Lifetime in Television*, recounts his journey to becoming a pioneer in nonfiction television, and how he created some of the longest-running, culture-shaping unscripted series in television history. He is the recipient of dozens of industry awards, including being honored as one of *Variety*'s "Titans of Unscripted TV," inducted into the *Realscreen* Awards Hall of Fame, and awarded *Broadcasting & Cable*'s "Producer of the Year."
>
> With more than two hundred shows for over fifty networks, under his leadership, A. Smith & Co. essentially forged the modern food competition reality genre in the United States with the launch of FOX's longest-running reality show, *Hell's Kitchen*, which has since spawned numerous projects, starring Chef Gordon Ramsay. Smith's flagship summer primetime show, NBC's *American Ninja Warrior*, has garnered seven Primetime Emmy® Award nominations. Earlier genre-

spanning successes include *Kitchen Nightmares*, *The Titan Games with Dwayne Johnson*, *Trading Spaces*, and *I Survived a Japanese Game Show*, while his eclectic array of series includes *Floor Is Lava*, *Mental Samurai*, *Welcome to Plathville*, and the NFL's *Pro Bowl Games*. Discover more at ASmithCo.com.

CHAPTER 17:

Go with Your Gut

LIZ LACHMAN

Ever find yourself stuck on a project or endeavor? You're going around and around, unsure of what to do? I have. Plenty of times.

When that happens, I've had to remind myself to check in with my gut. The gut is the "boss" and the brain is the "secretary." But I was taught the opposite, which has often left me on a hamster wheel, unable to make a decision.

It's not that my decisions have always worked out, but it does feel like it's the right path to take at the time. And one thing to know: I will deal with whatever comes after.

One of the best examples is my recent film, *Susan Feniger FORKED*, where I took footage I shot from the opening of Susan's restaurant Street, her first solo venture, and turned it into a documentary feature film about hope and resilience with the backdrop of the food industry.

For the longest time, I told myself that I didn't want to make this film. The main reason: it was a documentary and, as my passion has always been to make narrative films, I did not want to be known as a documentary filmmaker. However, during the pandemic, I was looking for a good project. I had the footage I'd shot when the restaurant opened in 2009, and I finally listened to my gut: "Don't be an idiot. Put it together and see what happens."

The gut is the *knowing*, the brain is the *doing*. Once I made the decision to make *Susan Feniger FORKED*, my brain helped me take the next steps to get it done.

The film has allowed me to hone my skills, and it didn't matter what type of movie it was. And it's worked out beautifully. We've traveled all over the country screening and promoting *Susan Feniger FORKED* in festivals. Even more importantly, I've made something I can be very proud of.

It was a good decision…that I made when I finally just allowed my gut, and not my brain, to take charge. I am now working on my next narrative project—expanding one of my short films into a full-length feature—and I couldn't be happier about it! Now let me get back on my hamster wheel, so I can get things done. *Kidding!*

Liz Lachman is an award-winning writer and director. Her screenplays have placed in the top percentages of the Nicholl Fellowships, Page Awards, and Final Draft Screenplay competitions. Her films have played at over eighty festivals around the world, garnering more than thirty awards. Learn more at LizLachman.com and ForkedtheFilm.com.

CHAPTER 18:

Be Prepared and Be Kind

JAMIE PACHINO

Be prepared is self-explanatory, but the more you prep for a meeting, pitch, or job interview, the more respect you are going to gain from anyone you are meeting/pitching/interviewing with. It demonstrates that you're professional, you're invested, you care, and that you will show up that way in the future. It creates confidence in the person you are meeting with, but also in yourself, because you know you've got (most) of the answers in your back pocket.

Being kind comes from my long experience working in writers' rooms for television series. When a showrunner (the boss/creator of the show) is putting together a room of writers for their staff, that person knows you will be in cramped quarters and stressful situations during some very long days while you're putting episodes together. You will also be on set with the cast and crew for weeks, in even more potentially stressful situations and through very long days. One of the top qualities a showrunner is seeking is your kindness and your empathy. They want to know that you can be a generous team player, and a source of kindness during those tense times.

Being kind comes from a lesson I learned early on, when I had just graduated from college with a degree in acting and moved to Chicago to start my career. There was another student in our class who was an incredible singer and dancer who moved to Chicago at the same time. This actor was cast right away in every single theatre in town—*but only once*. The actor was never hired again by *any* theatres because they were such a tremendous pain to work with. Eventually, that actor had to leave town to find other work. The lesson landed for me: be someone people want to work with twice, three times, or more. So much of that comes from your behavior—your kindness, openness, and empathy.

Jamie Pachino is an executive producer who writes series television (Hulu, Netflix, Amazon, Disney+, ABC, CBS, NBC, AMC, USA, TNT), film (DreamWorks, Disney, Lionsgate) and teleplays (Amazon, Hallmark, Lifetime). She is consulting producer for ABC's *Dr. Odyssey* and executive producer for Hulu's *All's Fair*, both for Ryan Murphy. Plus, Jamie has a screenplay optioned with River Road, called *Masterpiece*. She is also a playwright whose work has been commissioned, published, awarded, and produced all over the world. JamiePachino.com.

CHAPTER 19:

Treat People Like Family

DR. JAIME MORIGUCHI

My mom and dad instilled in me: Treat people the way you want to be treated. I'm a physician, so there are other rules I have to follow too.

I come from a small community in Hawaii. My town had only 2,500 people; because it was so small, we left our doors open, no one stole from each other, and we always felt safe. I feel very blessed having come from a good family.

My interest in medicine started when I was in high school. I remember being in pig lab; I was fascinated with the heart. It wasn't just the anatomy and physiology; I was amazed by how God put us all together. Physicians try to fix things, or at least try to make things better.

When I got the chance to go to Stanford, I started at the bottom. *We didn't even have calculus in high school.* I had the motivation to succeed, so I worked very hard and caught up. By the time I graduated, I was in the top 10–20 percent of my class. I went to UCLA for medical school and have been in Los Angeles ever since.

To be a doctor, you have to be goal-oriented and highly motivated early on. It's nonstop. If you don't concentrate, you will not get very far. You have to be the best you can be.

While our program for advanced heart disease is considered one of the top groups in the country—we do transplants, research, education—half of my practice is private patients. I get as much joy from taking care of them as I get from national recognition.

At the California Heart Center, we really care about our patients. Heart transplant patients are a special group. I want to be able to go to sleep at night knowing I did the best I can.

These people come to me and trust me with their health and their life. The least I can do is treat them like family.

> Dr. Jaime Moriguchi is the medical director of the Mechanical Circulatory Support Program for Advanced Heart Disease at Cedars-Sinai. He is also a private cardiologist.

CHAPTER 20:

Be Able to Look at Yourself in the Mirror

CHEF ROSSI

When you look at yourself in the mirror, do you wince a little bit? I'm not talking about your physical appearance; we all size ourselves up once in a while. Do you feel like you are a good person or someone who has done some bad things?

You might have a billion dollars in the bank and have trouble looking at yourself. Or you might be working for minimum wage, but have made countless people happy; you've changed lives. You've lived a life where you understand that it's not all about you, and you've made an impact.

I love being a caterer in New York. I've been doing this for thirty-six years, catered more than two thousand weddings, and won all sorts of awards. But what I love is bumping into my couples, which happens all the time. Whether it's the bank teller, a man who works in an antique store, or walking through the park, they're always so happy to see me. They're like, "Chef Rossi, you catered our wedding eighteen years ago, twenty years ago." People are still raving about the food, and that really makes my heart smile.

This has also been happening with my book, *The Punk Rock Queen of the Jews*, which is my wild, queer coming-of-age story. There's a young woman who's been messaging me, saying that the book really changed her life. She was feeling kind of sad, depressed, and lonely, and it was a story she really needed to read. It's given her hope, and she doesn't feel as alone.

You know how, with climate change, we talk a lot about your carbon footprint. Of course that's important, we don't want to hurt the earth, but there's also your footprint of the heart.

Are you going through this world, climbing the ladder and trying to become richer and more powerful, not caring how many people you've hurt?

The secret to success is to make a giant footprint, much larger than yourself. Leave a vast amount of love with the people you've helped and adored, who love and adore you.

Rossi is the director, owner, and executive chef of The Raging Skillet, a cutting-edge catering company known for breaking any and all rules. She's penned two memoirs, *The Raging Skillet* and *The Punk Rock Queen of the Jews*. Rossi has also written two full-length plays, a number of one-act comedies, and a one-woman stage adaptation of *The Punk Rock Queen of the*

Jews. She hosts the *Raging and Eating* podcast. Find out more at TheRagingSkillet.com.

CHAPTER 21:

Know Your Stuff

TRACIE THOMS

People think acting is easy because the good people make it look easy.

What actors do is literally impossible. It's subjective and mysterious. We're pretending to be other people, which is very hard to achieve. Yet people often think that, when we get up on stage, we wing it! No one would ever think a violin player or a ballerina was just "winging it."

To make anything look effortless, you have to train. This doesn't just apply to acting.

Don't just depend on your winning personality or your spunk or whatever. Take the time to learn as much as you can about the thing you want to do. If nothing else, it gives you confidence moving forward. Whatever challenges you face, you know you can depend on yourself, because you have the tools, the skills, and the education.

I was in a movie, and there were eight of us in this very emotional scene. We had to do it all day long, and there were only two of us who could do it over and over. We were the ones who had training. I remember the others asking, "How do you do it?"

"We're not up here, going on a whim, hoping that it comes to us," I said. "We know how to build it and sustain it, and the technical aspects of it. Because of that, we can do take after take after take."

This was relatively early in my career, and I remember thinking, "Thank God I spent the extra four years going to Juilliard for grad school."

As actors, you always want to trust your instincts first. Training is there for when your instincts fail. If you get lost, instead of spinning out, you can recenter yourself. You know all the building blocks: how you build a character, how you break the scene apart, how you do your script analysis. Because I had those tools, and I knew how to use them, I was able to do that difficult scene all day long.

No matter what your career, when you have the training and the credentials, and you keep honing your skills through classes and workshops, it sets you apart. I have friends who had training who are not that successful, and others for whom the opposite is true.

I am logical, but also a dreamer; you have to be in this business. Because of my Type A personality, I did everything by the book, and that has helped me. The key to this business is to stay diversified. I've worked in theatre, TV, and film.

When you know your stuff, word gets around. People call you in and hire you, because you have a reputation for being able to deliver.

> Tracie Thoms is a TV, film, and stage actor, best known for starring as Joanne Jefferson in *Rent* and Lily in *The Devil Wears Prada*. She has a recurring role as Karen Wilson on *9-1-1*.
>
> Born and raised in Baltimore, Maryland, Tracie began studying acting when she was nine years old. She attended the Baltimore School for the Arts, Howard University, where she earned a BFA, and then the Juilliard School, where she completed a postgraduate diploma in acting.
>
> Her resume includes a multitude of TV roles, including as series regular Desiree, along with Octavia Spencer, on the Apple series *Truth Be Told*, Magandra McGinty on *Wonderfalls*, Sasha from *As If*, and Kat Miller on *Cold Case*. She has appeared on *Station 19* (recurring), *Queen Sugar*, *Love, Victor*, and many others. *Jerry & Marge Go Large*, *Yes Day*, and *A Typical Wednesday* are just a few of her recent films.
>
> Tracie made her Broadway debut in Regina Taylor's *Drowning Crow*. Other Broadway credits include *Stick Fly* and *Falsettos*. In addition to appearing in several off-Broadway and regional productions, on July 18, 2008, she joined the final cast of *Rent*, starting July 26, 2008, reprising the character of Joanne; the performance was made into a DVD, *Rent: Filmed Live on Broadway*. Follow @TracieThoms on Instagram.

CHAPTER 22:

Never Dream Harder Than You Work

CHEF KATIE CHIN

In order to be truly successful in life, you have to do the work.

Sometimes people get so caught up in their dreams—excited, distracted, and fixated on the outcome—that they don't put their nose to the grindstone, and that is a recipe for defeat.

In this age of social media, people can become famous for becoming famous. That's the exception, not the rule.

Obviously, there's an actual trajectory toward becoming a doctor or a lawyer. Professions like these require you to get the degrees, gain the credibility or notoriety, and so forth.

However, in entrepreneurial or more creative fields, the path is a little less clear. In order to become successful and actually be taken seriously, you have to do whatever it takes: the research, the homework, the actual work. Walk the walk, talk the talk, and earn the street cred.

When I decided to become a caterer, it was hard for me to go from being an executive in Hollywood to lugging leaking bags of garbage up the stairs. But I felt like I couldn't take myself seriously until I actually did what it took to become a chef. I didn't go to culinary school; I was self-taught, like my mother, restaurateur Leann Chin, so I always felt like I had even more to prove.

I became especially motivated when my mom was sick with cancer. I set out to cook every single recipe in her cookbook with her on the phone, guiding me through each one. That was perhaps the best education.

Now, not only do I have credibility with others—whether it's going on a live television show, like *The Kelly Clarkson Show*, or being considered by a publisher for a cookbook—I also have an inner confidence. I know that I'm capable, and that I'm deserving of certain opportunities and accolades. It's like an internal engine that keeps me going.

We're constantly growing and learning; we're students of life. If anybody says, "I know everything," then they're fooling themselves, because things are constantly moving. Whether you are a chef, a consultant, an entrepreneur, or even an electrical engineer, you have to keep learning. That way you can soar in your chosen profession.

CHAPTER 22: NEVER DREAM HARDER THAN YOU WORK

Celebrity chef Katie Chin, Wok Star Catering, is an award-winning cookbook author, caterer, and playwright. Her books include *Katie Chin's Global Family Cookbook*, *300 Best Rice Cooker Recipes*, and *Everyday Thai Cooking*, as well as *Everyday Chinese Cooking*, which she wrote with her mother, restaurateur Leann Chin. The duo also co-hosted the national PBS cooking series *Double Happiness*.

After growing up working in the kitchens of her late mother's award-winning Minneapolis-area restaurants, Chin moved to LA after college to pursue a career in film and television marketing. Her passion for cooking was reignited when her mother came to her rescue after realizing her daughter had forgotten how to cook. Leann hopped on a plane with frozen shrimp in her carry-on, on a mission to teach Katie how to cook again. After they threw a series of dinner parties together, Katie quit her job as a film marketing executive, and the rest is history. Chin's one-woman show is called *Holy Shitake! A Wok Star is Born*. ChefKatieChin.com.

CHAPTER 23:

Be Ready!

KEVIN DANIELS

I find myself to be a student of "Yes."

Always put yourself in a position where you're ready and available for whatever blessing comes knocking. It's so easy to get distracted or be hard on yourself, especially when working toward long-term goals. Stay physically and mentally present for whatever the universe has in store for you.

Are you into yoga? Is it hiking? Do you go to the gym?

I have a routine. I do my affirmations. I pray. I do a lot of journaling to capture and collect my thoughts. I move my body. I do whatever I feel will help me be ready for whatever presents itself.

My grandmother used to say something that really stuck with me: "In this moment, you have everything you need. And life is just a series of moments."

As an actor, often, I'll get a phone call. "So-and-so mentioned you. We need you on set in Canada tomorrow. Can you go?" Yes!

One time, I was at a bar with a friend, and he told me he was doing a fundraiser for a theatre company. He asked if I would do a couple of scenes for it; a five-minute performance. I did it, and it was a great night.

During the event, the artistic director asked me, "Why don't you do theatre anymore?" And I responded, "Well, I do theatre. It's just not as lucrative, and I've been working a lot in TV." So, he said, "If we could find a play, would you consider doing it?" I said, "You know what, absolutely. If you find a play, and I read it and love it, we'll talk."

He tricked me. Little did I know, he already had a play with me in mind. He sent it to me the next day. We read it together, and I fell for the script. It was a ninety-seven-page play, called *Monsters in American Cinema*, about grief, manhood, and growing up. It was very funny and touching.

I ended up doing this beautiful play for two months. And it was all because I said yes to doing a two-page scene for a fundraiser.

Actor Kevin Daniels's impressive career has spanned more than two decades. Seamlessly transitioning between theatre, TV, and film, he has captivated audiences with his authenticity, charisma, and talent.

Roles include Franklin, a police detective, alongside Ramon Rodriguez and Erika Christensen in the ABC procedural *Will Trent*; he also recurs as Tiny on Paramount Plus's revival of *Frasier*. Other TV credits include *The Big Leap, Sirens, Modern Family, Atypical, Why Women Kill, AJ and the Queen*, and *Council of Dads*. Film credits include *Ladder 49, The Island, Hollywood Homicide, Raze, The Watcher*, and *aTypical Wednesday*.

After graduating from Juilliard, Kevin made his Broadway debut in Shakespeare's *Twelfth Night*. In 2012, Daniels played the lead role of Magic Johnson in Broadway's *Magic/Bird*. He recently appeared in *Masters of the America Cinema* at the Rogue Machine Theatre in Los Angeles.

Follow @KevinDaniels27 on Instagram.

BONUS CHAPTER:

Just Go

GREG GRUNBERG

One tip or one bit of advice that I have lived by when it comes to business is: hustle. Don't stop hustling. It is a numbers game. That's not to say that you should spread yourself too thin, but don't look at every opportunity as the Holy Grail. One opportunity will lead to another, which will lead to another. Work gets work.

Yes, there are projects and there are businesses that you should hold precious and you should work extra hard on, and everything that you do you should do 1,000 percent. However, as long as you're hustling and working and representing yourself in the best possible way each and every day, you will be rewarded in the end.

It goes back to what my dad, Gerry Grunberg, told me years ago, which was, "Just go." It sounds like the Nike slogan, but what my dad means is, if you have an opportunity to meet someone, who may not be the ultimate person you want to meet, "Just go." You never know what that meeting might lead to.

I have found that, more often than not, when there is an opportunity that I feel isn't perfect, I'm often shocked at how great it ultimately becomes.

As an actor, I can recall many times when an audition comes in and, by the description alone, I am not exactly perfect for the role. However, my representation tells me and my gut tells me, "Just go," because you never know where it's going to lead. And inevitably that producer, director, or casting director takes a liking to me, based on that audition. And, although I may not get the role, I do get something down the road, because they are familiar with me. One thing leads to another. But if you don't start with that one thing, it's never going to happen.

The other bit of advice that I can give people, whether in entertainment or in business, is to bet on yourself. No one is going to want to take a chance on you and be the first person to give you an opportunity. You need to be that person! You need to give yourself that opportunity, that big break. That way, the next person who has a chance to give you an opportunity or take a meeting with you knows that you've been there before, and someone else has already taken a chance on you…even though that person is you. Trust me, it makes sense.

> Greg Grunberg has been an actor for more than thirty years, in such projects as *Felicity, Alias, LOST, HEROES, Star Wars,* and *Star Trek*. He currently can be seen in *Duster* on HBO Max, premiering 2025. He is also philanthropic and co-created Talk

About It, an organization devoted to removing stigma and educating people on various conditions that need attention, such as epilepsy, as his oldest son is living well with the condition. TalkAboutItOnVideo.com.

PART 4 -

NETWORKING

The people you meet are your resources, partners, and champions. Your community grows every time you grow your community.

CHAPTER 24:

Leverage Your Network's Network

BRYNNE TILLMAN

The best way to get opportunities, professionally and personally, is through your network. Even fifteen or twenty years ago, we would go to events, meet people, and collect business cards. Then, we'd stick a rubber band around our pile of cards and put them in the corner of our desk. And, although we would follow up with some of these people, the networking wasn't as efficient as it could have been.

In 1992, I remember sitting across from a client, staring at his overflowing Rolodex, thinking, "If I could get a hold of that, I could see who he knows to ask for introductions, and I wouldn't have to cold-call anymore." But it wasn't exactly appropriate to say, "Mr. Client, can I thumb through your address book?"

Fast-forward a decade, and we were given the gift of LinkedIn. This powerful networking platform gave us the ability to search and filter our connections' connections and leverage our warm network to gain access to our targeted buyers.

You would no longer need to approach a client or a networking partner and say, "Here are all the great things I do. Who do you know that could use my services?" The response typically is a shrug and an, "I'm sorry, I can't think of anyone right now."

Instead of going prospecting one-on-one, you can now meet with networking partners, run a list of the people they are connected to that you'd like to meet, and get either introductions or permission to name-drop.

Here's how it works:

Before a meeting with a client or networking partner, connect with them on LinkedIn and search for their connections. Build a list of eight to ten to twelve people they're connected to that you would like to know. **Bonus:** Invite them to do the same with your connections.

Now, when you meet, rather than asking, "Who do you know?" you can say, "I hope you don't mind, but I identified a few people in your network that I'd love to get in front of. Can I run these names by you?"

Eight, ten, or twelve people might become two or three meaningful introductions. This is a huge time-saver for prospecting and networking, and it is way more fun.

I had a client, Rob Petcove, who owned a benefits company, and I noticed he was connected to Rob Curley at TD Bank. Rob Curley is someone I had been trying to get in to see for a year, and there was no response. Everyone was prospecting Rob Curley.

So I asked Rob Petcove, "How do you know Rob Curley?" He said, "Both our boys have juvenile diabetes, and we've been in the same group since they were three. He's a great guy."

After I told him I'd been trying to get to see him forever, Rob Petcove said he'd make a quick email introduction. I was still in Rob's office when I got a reply from Rob Curley: "Monday morning noon. Here's the address."

I'm like, *Wait! What just happened?*

I arrived twenty minutes early, all excited. When I walked in, he was sitting at his desk with his arms crossed, leaning back in his chair. He said, "Go."

"Why am I here?" I asked.

"Because Rob Petcove told me I should meet with you, and I'll do anything he asks," he replied.

I was mid-sentence, telling him "If I can show your bankers how to get in meetings with LinkedIn…" when he stopped me. He offered me a date on the calendar (their next team meeting), asked how long I needed (half a day), and booked me before even asking my rate.

I closed the fastest deal I ever closed with the prospect that took the longest to get in front of, and it only took a warm introduction to get there.

Remember, it's not just about the ask. It's also about how you help the people in your network. If you don't have networking partners, ask your clients who are the other trusted advisors. If they say they work with a specific CPA, ask if they would be open to making an introduction or if you can reach out to them and introduce yourself. Even when you introduce yourself, you're at a higher level of credibility since you share a client. You can feel more comfortable introducing them into your network and vice versa. But if the client says, "I don't really like my CPA," then you can offer them an introduction to any of the CPAs in your network that your clients love.

When getting these referrals, your number one goal is for the prospect to thank the person who referred you for making the introduction, because you brought so much value into their world. When you do that, you'll have unlimited referrals and people will want to work with you.

> Brynne Tillman is CEO of Social Sales Link and co-founder of The Modern Banker. She helps professionals start more trust-based conversations on LinkedIn without being salesy. Learn more at SocialSalesLink.com.

CHAPTER 25:

Attend Networking Events with a Plan

LIZ HEIMAN

As an introvert, I find networking events to be way out of my comfort zone. Yet, when I approach them with a plan, they are not only manageable, but beneficial.

Before I go to any event, I gather as much information as I can. That starts with trying to find out who is going to be there. If it's on Meetup, they list the attendees. Conferences will have lists of speakers and sponsors; same with trade shows. And sometimes you can go on LinkedIn and see who is posting about attending.

Then, I'll make a plan for who I want to meet or have a conversation with while I am there, and what I want to talk to them about. I am great at building strong relationships and having serious conversations with prospects and clients. I'm absolutely intent on solving their problems, and if I'm not the right person, I will find the right resource for them. However, I'm not really good at starting conversations. I don't do small talk well, so I've had to learn how to chat about the weather before diving into important matters.

When I arrive at the event, I start looking around the room: What is everyone doing? Who's talking to whom? How are they standing? How welcoming is that group? Why is that person in the corner, alone, staring at their appetizer?

I usually make a point of talking to the people who are by themselves first. They're typically very interesting people, who are also introverts and don't know how to join the other groups. I immediately walk over to them, while keeping an eye out for the people on my wish list.

When it becomes appropriate, I'll excuse myself from the conversation and make my way to talk to those I previously identified.

Some people can walk into a room and automatically everyone goes to them; they are like magnets. You can tell they are comfortable in that situation. That is not true for me.

You can always tell when I enter an event I haven't planned for, because I walk in and don't have any idea what to do. Sometimes, if I haven't prepped, I'll be driving to an event and unconsciously start thinking about it: "If, okay, if Carol's there, we need to talk about this. And I have to remember to ask so-and-so about that." It's not ideal, but it does the job.

I need to walk into a room with purpose; I have to have a plan.

CHAPTER 25: ATTEND NETWORKING EVENTS WITH A PLAN

> Liz Heiman is the Sales Operating System Architect for and the founder of Regarding Sales. She guides leaders from what's often a random and chaotic sales process to a systematic and sustainable strategy that fills their prospect pipeline week in and week out. RegardingSales.com.

CHAPTER 26:

Commit to Conversations

LARRY LEVINE

I'm a massive believer that if you can't do the simple, little things correctly, you'll never be able to do the big things correctly. This is one of the simple things. I've held myself accountable for this when I worked in sales, and it is a process I have continued since I started Selling from the Heart.

Every day, I strive to:

- Make one new connection
- Drive one new conversation
- Have one conversation with someone inside my customer base

If you can do those three things, and you do them with discipline every single day, the math plays out. In the span of one month, you will have made thirty new connections, had thirty new conversations, and have spoken to thirty people inside your customer base.

When salespeople add one new connection to their network every single day and hold themselves accountable to having one new conversation a day, that alone creates sales sustainability over time. When you layer in the last goal, which is to have a conversation with a customer every day, it takes things to a game-changing level.

Typical sales teams tend to go for the low-hanging fruit (easy conversations/easy sales). Most are not going what I call high, wide, and deep within their customer base.

Look at all the people that are either key decision-makers or influencers that are in your customer base. When you get beyond who you know and have conversations with those you don't know, you will instantaneously start creating sales opportunities.

I love seeing salespeople's eyes just light up, and the resulting successes, when they discover valuable connections in the companies they already serve. For example, "I didn't realize that Jane Doe was inside ABC Company. As I got to know Jane, I uncovered some of the issues and challenges that she has in her position/department. When I explained how my product/service will help, it created a winning scenario."

One of my favorite authors is Dr. Henry Cloud. I just finished reading one of his older books, *Integrity*, and this ties right in. Chapter 10 is called "Eating Problems for Breakfast." And Dr. Cloud writes, "If you cannot uncover problems, you will not uncover profit."

When you're having conversations with your current customers, don't just think of those you always go to—the warm friendlies. Find somebody you do not know and discover the problems they may be having. That directly ties to profit.

Just by doing those simple little things, every single day, you'd uncover well over seven hundred new conversations in the span of a year.

> Larry Levine is the international bestselling author of two books, *Selling from the Heart* and *Selling in a Post-Trust World*, and the co-host of the award-winning *Selling from the Heart Podcast*. Larry believes people would rather do business with a sales professional who sells from the heart, as opposed to a sales rep who is an empty suit. Blending a heart of service with over three decades of in-the-field sales experience, Larry helps sales teams leverage the power of authenticity to grow revenue, grow themselves, and enhance the lives of their clients. SellingfromtheHeart.net.

CHAPTER 27:

Find the Whos for Your Hows

DAVE SANDERSON

To succeed in business and life, you must embrace uncertainty. If you want to go to places you have never been and succeed beyond your wildest dreams, you must step out of your comfort zone, work hard, and be resilient.

Uncertainty ignites opportunity, which transforms your life. But you don't need to do it alone.

Find the whos for your hows. You have a goal: that's a how. Now, who can help you get to that how?

When I started my little company, I was doing much of the work. I'm good at sales and revenue, but terrible at accounts receivable, payables, and that sort of thing. I was letting people not pay me for months. I needed someone to run operations. I found a who for my how when I hired Lisa as my operations manager. My company started doing double the revenue, and it's now on the way to ten times where I started.

One of the most important whos for your how is a mentor. Find someone who has walked their talk, and you can reduce the time it takes to reach your goals. You can seek out mentors in your industry, reach out to people you admire online, and even learn from mentors throughout history.

If I need a tip on leadership, I'll read about Abraham Lincoln and how he led during a crisis. If I need information about how to communicate more effectively, I'll read about Ronald Reagan; he was a great communicator. If I have a legal question, I have a retired superior court judge I can call. I reached out to motivational speaker and author Simon Sinek (*Find Your Why*) to tell him how much I loved his TED talk. When he replied, he told me I could text him anytime.

I met my first mentor shortly after I moved to Charlotte, North Carolina, in the early 1980s. I was a second assistant restaurant manager at a place called Howard Johnson's, and I worked the second and third shift. There was a seventy-seven-year-old gentleman who would come in with his wife every night. His name was Bill. He wore a flannel shirt and drove a pickup truck; he'd have ice cream and coffee, and we'd talk.

One night, I told him that I had just started to date the woman who would become my wife, but I had no money. He gave me a couple of movie passes and said, "Take her out on me. Tell me how it goes."

The guy at the movie theatre said to send his regards to Bill, which I did the next day. Turns out, Bill owned that movie theatre; he'd owned eighty movie theatres and restaurants in the Carolinas since the 1920s. He was a multimillionaire. Bill said, "Let me show you what it's going to take to be successful." For thirteen years he mentored me, until he passed away.

My dad taught me that you don't have to be a member of every club. You just have to know somebody who is a member.

Find your whos. It'll make facing uncertainty much easier when you have support along the way.

> Dave Sanderson is a nationally recognized leadership speaker, accomplished author, and inspirational survivor of what is known as "The Miracle on the Hudson." As the last passenger off US Airways Flight 1549, which had to ditch into the river, he took the lessons he learned from that profound experience in the frigid water and emerged from the wreckage with a mission to encourage others to do the right thing and to share coping skills to address any adversity they may face. DaveSandersonSpeaks.com.

CHAPTER 28:

Begging Never Helped a Relationship

DAVE BRICKER

One sure way to put an end to a relationship on the rocks is to beg someone to take you back. And begging a prospect to marry you before you even ask their name looks lonely, pathetic, and a bit creepy.

So why do so many marketers start begging before the relationship even starts?

- "Hi. Are you looking for an app developer?"
- "Click here for a free SEO analysis of your website."
- "Fill your coaching calendar with qualified leads."
- "Hey, you. Would you buy my stuff?"

Who are these people?

My friend Maria, a web designer, found herself competing with cheap crowdsourcing sites that charged overseas rates. Initially, her marketing efforts failed. She'd reach out to hundreds of prospects, offer her services, and lose the race as soon as the conversation turned to costs.

On the advice of her business mentor, she changed tactics. Instead of begging people to buy websites, she began to publish weekly articles, stories, and tips that helped her readers understand the value of a trained designer. The business leaders in her articles understood that good design is an investment, not an expense. Those who tried to save money ended up with cliché solutions that felt "safe," but failed to expand their brands or grow their businesses. In these articles, the closest she came to asking for anything was her small website link at the bottom with an invitation to connect.

The effort took some time, but eventually, Maria began to receive inquiries from professionals who were ready to focus on "big picture" business goals and on how the right combination of design and technology could help them succeed. They thanked her for the value and perspective she'd given them in her posts and treated her as a trusted consultant who could make them money.

Cost became an afterthought. Maria was able to quadruple her prices; the results she produced exceeded her fees. And that old, awkward pricing conversation turned into, "Send me a proposal and we'll get started."

When Maria stopped looking hungry, desperate, and focused on herself, it made her approachable. She offered value to everyone, whether they became clients or not, and this inspired ideal prospects to connect, respect, and reciprocate.

Business success depends on fostering warm, trusting relationships. Ask them their name, what they care about, and what conflicts they face. Tell them you can offer a solution (only if you have one), and then *wait until they ask for it* before sharing it.

Don't be that bad date who talks about themselves all evening (until their prearranged fake emergency phone call gives them an excuse to end the evening with a fake apology). Ask. Listen. Engage.

> Dave Bricker is a speaker, author, transatlantic adventure sailor, and business storytelling expert. If you want to say it, share it, or sell it, bring him your story; he'll help you tell it. Connect with Dave Bricker at Speakipedia.com, the world's most comprehensive resource for speaking and storytelling.

CHAPTER 29:

Use "Windows," Not "Doorway," Thinking

MICHAEL RODERICK

Most of the time, when we are presented with any problem, there is one solution that feels like it makes the most sense. The problem is that everyone else is often thinking the same thing. Since most people are going through that same door, it's really crowded. In windows thinking, I like to look at all of the "windows" of the situation, rather than the door that everyone else is going through.

Let's say there's someone whose work you admire that you want to meet, and they are going to be at a conference. The doorway thinking is to go to the conference and try to catch them after they speak on stage. The problem is that a lot of other people are also going to want to do the same thing, and you could end up in a really long line.

Windows thinking leads to the question, "If everyone wants to meet this person after they speak, what are the other opportunities to meet them?"

So, make a list of windows:

- You could see if anyone else you know is going to be speaking at the conference, and, if so, ask if they could host a breakfast or a dinner and invite the person you admire to attend.
- You could ask the conference organizer about the timing of the speaking event and see if you're allowed to be in the room early, before the speaker goes onstage, to try to catch them before.
- You could reach out to that person before the conference and ask if they'd be open to meeting up there or coming to another event you are hosting.

These are just a few "windows" of opportunity. Even more digging would lead to additional ideas of ways to connect.

After the experience, and testing the different windows, then look at which practice worked best. Those are the ones to implement more in the future.

When I was raising money for Broadway shows, one of the most common models was to do an industry reading. The way it worked was that you would prep for twenty-nine hours and then invite producers, investors, and potential partners to see the show. The doorway thinking approach was that this was always a gamble, because you could have a ton of investors and producers RSVP and then have almost everyone cancel at the last minute.

One time, I had a show where I had fifteen members of the industry scheduled to attend, and the day of the reading only two showed up. After that, I decided to use windows thinking instead. I asked myself, "What is the one reason someone, like a producer or investor, would make sure to show up to a reading?" I realized that, if they were invited as a guest, they could always drop out at the last minute. However, if they were invited as a panelist, it looked really bad if they didn't show up.

Here's how I tested it. I created a panel of investors and producers; I asked them to come to a reading and then share at the end why they would or would not invest in the show. Not only did the panelists all show up, but the room filled with other producers and investors who wanted to meet the folks on the panel.

By using windows thinking, I ended up with record numbers of industry leaders attending my reading.

> Michael Roderick is the CEO of Small Pond Enterprises, which helps thoughtful givers become thought leaders by making their brands referable, their messaging memorable, and their ideas unforgettable. Michael's unique methodology comes from his own experience of going from being a high school English teacher to a Broadway producer in under two years. Michael uses Broadway-informed branding techniques to helps his clients find their I.F. (Innovative Framework) and create offers where they get paid for their brains. SmallPondEnterprises.com.

CHAPTER 30:

Visibility = Opportunity

BOBBIE CARLTON

Many people tell me they are interested in more opportunities to speak onstage, but I would suggest they tend to think too narrowly about "speaking" and its outcomes. Instead, think about how you can drive visibility and how this can impact your business, your career, or your life. Every time we get visible, we have opportunities, if we are willing, able, and prepared to capitalize on them.

Visibility can be a speaking engagement, winning an award, being a mentor for an event or accelerator, being a judge at a contest, and more. You can write an article, be a guest on a podcast, or appear as an expert source on radio or TV. You want people to see you in action. Every time they see you in action, you are able to generate trust and credibility, and demonstrate why they should engage further with you.

In addition, many people don't realize the size of the opportunity they have when they share their expertise as a speaker at an event. Some speakers will turn away all nonpaid speaking events, or events with smaller audiences, but others will take a broader view, assessing each opportunity with an eye peeled for the correct audiences.

Even a smaller room can provide rich returns:

Is your target customer in the room? No? Is the marketing for the event capable of reaching your target audience? Often the speakers are the centerpiece of an event's marketing campaign. You could be gaining important visibility through the event's email marketing, social media campaigns, and on the event website.

Could your target audience hear about you from the people in the room? Even if your audience isn't directly in the room, you still may have a chance of making an impression through a connection made at the event.

Then, add on the key connections you could potentially be making in the green room or speakers' lounge. Many people dismiss panel invitations as not worthy of their time, missing the opportunity to mingle with other VIPs.

> Bobbie Carlton is the founder of three companies, Carlton PR & Marketing, Innovation Nights, and Innovation Women, an online "visibility bureau," dedicated to providing women and other underrepresented voices with a chance to be seen as thought leaders and experts. InnovationWomen.com.

BONUS CHAPTER:

Create Your Own Community

JESSIE-SIERRA ROSS

At age five, I knew I wanted to be a professional ballet dancer. I chased that goal, and, when I was fourteen, I became a professional, dancing with various companies in the New England area with great stars from all over the world.

Even when I was dancing professionally, I was focused on the future. My backup plan was to teach, so I developed skills that led to choreography and coaching. These are all elements I translated into my career as a blogger, stylist, photographer, and media personality in the food space.

One of the biggest influences, however, was community. I was part of a huge dance community. When I decided to take the leap and become a full-time food content creator, I quickly realized I need to meet all the people in that area, so I could create interconnections. This included not only food blogging and food photography, but also food stylists, chefs, mixologists, authors, and agents, throughout the world.

But what happens when you can't quite find a community that fits your needs? You create your own.

Find a platform that you're comfortable sharing on, and start small. Whether on social media, through message boards, or via scheduled Zooms, people are looking to connect. I started by bringing in a handful of creator friends for weekly chats. They, in turn, brought their creative friends. *Like-minded people tend to find each other!* Word spread about our safe and supportive space that allowed people to connect and learn. What started as a twenty-person food blogger group exploded to more than two thousand food and photography industry members within a year.

It's a small world. It's a very small world. With the generation of dancers that I grew up in, I can walk into any sort of dance event and know three people in the audience, because it's so tight. We had the same teachers, the same choreographers, and the same experiences. And I think that translates pretty much into any niche.

If you are working toward being a trailblazer in any area, bring your people together. From connections to advice, sharing goals, and commiserating over common frustrations, being part of a creator community can make such a difference. Develop friendships, start collaborations, and learn from each other. And look down below and see who's coming up, and see how you can help them move forward too.

Jessie-Sierra Ross is a cookbook author, television contributor, and food and lifestyle blogger at *Straight to the Hips, Baby*. Jessie-Sierra's cooking and home entertaining book, *Seasons Around the Table*, includes seasonal menus, original food and drink recipes, floral table decor, and modern home entertaining tutorials.

A native Bostonian and former professional ballerina, Jessie-Sierra traded in her fast-paced urban life for the farm-to-table landscape of western Massachusetts. A self-taught cook and avid home entertainer, she brings her unique artistic background to her light and bright food photography style and recipe approach.

With ongoing appearances on NBC, CBS, and PBS stations, Jessie-Sierra has become one of the region's popular "how-to" food and home entertaining specialists. Whether it's sharing her recipes on her blog or live on television, Jessie-Sierra's goal is to empower the home cook to create their own food experiences for family and friends. Follow @straighttothehipsbaby on Instagram or visit straighttothehipsbaby.com.

PART 5 -

COMMUNICATION

Being able to craft and express ideas puts you in a position of power.

CHAPTER 31:

Be Able to Say What You Do in Three Words

DAYNA STEELE

If someone asks you that magic "What do you do" question, and you say, "I'm a speaker and an author," they're going to say, "That's nice," put in their AirPods, and tune you out. When I tell strangers/new friends, "I create rock stars," it's the start of a conversation.

When you sit next to someone on an airplane and they ask you what you do, can you articulate your response in a simple, effective manner? The more specific you can be with what you do, what you want to achieve, and what you need to get there, the better your chances of accomplishing your goals.

Early on, I set my sights on being a rock 'n' roll DJ.

My goal went from, "I want to be on the radio in Houston" to "I want to be on the radio at KLOL, the station I grew up listening to."

After I got that job, I wanted a full-time job on the air. Then, I wanted to be on the air during the day when people were actually awake. My next goals: wanting to be the highest-paid, highest-rated woman DJ and then wanting to be the highest-paid, highest-rated of all DJs (male and female).

I achieved each and every one of those goals.

When you are specific, aspirational, and able to articulate what you are working toward, you are more likely to get everything you need to make that happen.

Here's an exercise I like to do with people. I ask them to give me a word-vomit, mishmash paragraph, explaining what they do and what they really want to do. Then I tell them to clean it up into three concise sentences. Next, pare it down to one sentence. Finally, put it into three words.

You want your three words to initiate the question, "What does that mean?"

For example, my nephew is an engineer; he specializes in finding out what could possibly go wrong after someone creates or designs an engineering project.

The three words he came up with are: "I break things."

I told him, "That's perfect!"

Now, the conversation on the airplane goes something like this:

"What do you do?"

He says, "I break things."

"Are you in demolition?"

"I find what could possibly go wrong with a product, and I reverse-engineer it."

"What have you worked on?"

"I've worked on these design projects."

And the conversation evolves from there.

When you say to someone, "I just want a new job," "I want my big break," or "I am willing to do anything," they don't know where to start to help you. It actually makes their brain freeze and explode at the same time.

When you can express something really specific, they can immediately put themselves in the helper role. They can picture in their mind who they know and how they can help you get a leg up to achieving your goals.

> Dayna Steele is a Texas rock radio Hall of Famer, the creator of the *101 Ways to Rock* self-help book series, a serial entrepreneur, a popular business speaker, actor, playwright, caregiver, and activist. Having lost her mother to Alzheimer's, Dayna is now a leading voice for Alzheimer's caregivers. She authored *Surviving Alzheimer's with Friends, Facebook,*

and a Really Big Glass of Wine and created the dark dementia comedy, *The Woman in the Mirror*. The play, based on her experience navigating her mother's Alzheimer's with the support of friends and strangers on Facebook, blends therapy, sanity, laughter, and wine, showcasing Dayna's resilience and creativity. Dayna can be heard weekdays from ten a.m. to two p.m. Central on the Houston Radio Platinum app and on her two podcasts, *Surviving Alzheimer's* and *Dayna's Diner Podcast*. Learn more at DaynaSteele.com.

CHAPTER 32:

Preach What You Practice

VIVEKA VON ROSEN

I was on a call with my accountability partners, and one of them, my friend Clare, mentioned the concept of "Preach what you practice." I asked, "How's that different from practicing what you preach or walking your talk?" Turns out there is a subtle, but very real, difference.

Many of us hear of something great and turn around and share it with our networks (AI! Hair-growth shampoo! Intermittent fasting!). The problem is that many of the people we are influencing believe we have a genuine and thorough experience of the things we are sharing. They might spend money they don't really have on a "promised land" product or even hurt themselves or their businesses with an unproven solution.

That's why I now follow the essential rule of preaching on only what I practice myself. I don't blindly advocate for ideas, products, or services that I haven't used. I ensure that everything I promote comes from my personal experience and genuine belief. This enables me to establish credibility and trust with my audience and prevent potential harm to my reputation.

People often think they are being helpful when they pass along things that sound good: "Read this blog, buy this gadget, drink this magic drink." But that can cause real harm. However, preaching *only* what you practice promotes authenticity and consistency in your business.

For example...

When a friend introduced me to a product called Armra to help with my weak nails and thin hair, I initially wanted to share it with everyone. However, sticking to my "preach what you practice" rule meant that I needed to try the product myself before advocating for it. After using Armra for two and a half months and experiencing noticeable improvements, I felt confident in sharing my positive experiences with others. This authenticity helped my endorsement come across as more genuine and trustworthy.

Before I started preaching what I practice, I was trying to sell my own journal, but wasn't using it myself. This lack of authenticity led to poor sales, as my audience couldn't see the genuine value in the product. Once I reflected on the situation and discovered why I wasn't using my journal (it was bulky, hard to use, and too big), I reformatted it to better meet my personal needs. After using and genuinely loving the new version, I could confidently preach about it, leading to improved sales and customer satisfaction.

When you openly share your experiences and stand behind the products or services you endorse, your audience is more likely to trust your recommendations. This approach not only strengthens your credibility, but also encourages loyalty and engagement from your followers. By embodying the principles, practices, or products you preach, you create a strong foundation for your business based on honesty and integrity.

> Viveka von Rosen is dedicated to empowering successful female executives and entrepreneurs with their brand and business pivots. As an industry expert with over nineteen years of experience in LinkedIn marketing and sales, she is a recognized authority in the business world. An accomplished author and international speaker, Viveka captivates audiences with her keynote addresses on transition and transformation, catalyzing people to find their voices and create their own transformative and transformational ventures.
>
> Outside her professional pursuits, she embraces adventure, whether soaring the skies on hang gliders, exploring the ocean's depths through scuba diving, or hiking amidst the picturesque Colorado foothills and Costa Rican landscapes.
>
> Viveka's core message is "Women's Words will Change the World" and her mission is to empower her clients to bring their legacy dreams to life. BeyondtheDreamBoard.com.

CHAPTER 33:

Be Unapologetically Yourself in All Aspects of Your Business

M.J. FIEVRE

More than just a buzzword, authenticity is a powerful business philosophy that fosters trust, builds stronger relationships, and sets you apart in a crowded marketplace. When you're authentic, you attract the right people—clients, collaborators, and team members—who resonate with your true self. This authenticity extends to all areas of your business, from branding and marketing to daily interactions and decision-making processes. By staying true to who you are, you create a consistent and genuine presence that others can rely on.

In my journey as a writer and educator, I've found that authenticity has been a cornerstone of my success. For instance, when I was working on *Badass Black Girl*, I shared concerns and personal stories that were deeply vulnerable. This honesty and transparency allowed readers to connect with the material on a profound level, leading to stronger engagement and positive feedback.

Additionally, when speaking at events or conducting workshops, I make it a point to share my true self—my challenges, victories, and everything in between. This approach enhances my credibility and inspires others to embrace their authenticity, creating a ripple effect of genuine connections and growth. What you see is what you get.

> M.J. Fievre is the visionary behind Badass Black Girl, a brand dedicated to empowering and inspiring Black women. With an eye for impactful storytelling and a heart committed to fostering community and growth, M.J. is a celebrated author and entrepreneur who believes in the power of personalized engagement and strategic planning for business success. Her innovative approach to management and leadership has garnered widespread acclaim, making her a sought-after speaker and consultant in the realms of personal development and business excellence. MJFievre.com.

CHAPTER 34:

Shining Brightly

HOWARD BROWN

We all get knocked down in life, business, health, and relationships. The key is to get back up again and again.

And when you share your experience of resilience to uplift others, that's even better.

As a two-time stage IV cancer survivor, thirty years apart, I have been knocked down twice where my life came to a screeching halt. Putting yourself back together, like Humpty Dumpty, takes real work, emotionally, physically, financially, and in relationships. I woke up every day, choosing kindness, giving, gratitude, and offering and accepting compassion. I went through the healing process with grace and joy…mostly. Being intentional in this way helped me build my resiliency, the kind that is strong enough to overcome trauma. I let in the light of others until I could go back to shining brightly myself.

After my second stage IV colon cancer diagnosis, and resulting treatments, survivorship, and advocacy, I decided I wanted to leave a legacy of values and inspiration. During the COVID pandemic, I interviewed via Zoom the more than 150 people who were the most important, influential people in my life. Those conversations became the basis of my book *Shining Brightly: A memoir of resilience and hope by a two-time cancer survivor, Silicon Valley entrepreneur and interfaith peacemaker.*

A few months after the book's publication, I started the *Shining Brightly* podcast, where I interview guests who embody triumph over tragedy via human resolve and inspiration. The goal of the show is to provide a platform to share human stories of those who found the resilience to survive, strive, and thrive.

If you want to be a force multiplier for positive change, share your story and the stories of others. Use your social platform, whether it's a blog, podcast, or video, to shine more light into the world.

> Howard Brown, a.k.a. Mr. Shining Brightly, frequently appears wearing his signature white metallic sunglasses. He is a Silicon Valley entrepreneur, bestselling author of *Shining Brightly*, award-winning international speaker, inspirational podcaster, survivorship coach, and health technology consultant. He shares the keys to leading a resilient life with hope that drives successful community leaders, business innovators, and healthcare advocates. ShiningBrightly.com.

CHAPTER 35:

Think Big in Your Media Outreach

STACIA CRAWFORD

Whether you do this on your own or are working with a publisher, publicist, or booking agent, in setting up your media plan, think big.

Those who haven't necessarily been showing up in the media, or have just started considering media as part of their strategy for growing their business, tend to think local. They think having a little article in their community newspaper is enough. It's a great start. But that's all it is: a start!

I want you to think bigger! That's not to say you're going to be on *The Today Show* or *Good Morning America* tomorrow, but you need to understand that ultimately that is the goal.

The goal is to get high-level media attention, because the bigger the outlet, the bigger a credibility marker it is. You want to build that "know, like, and trust" factor in the people who you want to hire you or buy your product. Almost anyone can be in their local paper. When you say, "I've been featured on *Good Morning, America* and in *Vanity Fair* and *Oprah* magazine," now people are listening.

So often in our lives and in our businesses, we think in terms of increments. I'm going to take these baby steps from here to there. That's logical and necessary in certain realms. However, when you're thinking in terms of media and visibility, it doesn't necessarily always have to be from point A to point B. Sometimes, you can go from point A to point M.

That's how media works with the right stories. When you really understand what journalists are looking for, you can skip the line, so to speak. That means, see where your ultimate media goals lie and then reverse-engineer it.

Remember, though, it's going to be different for everybody. For example, if you're trying to sell tickets to a local event, that's going to be a whole different strategy from someone who's trying to sell books nationally or globally. When you are trying to reach people in a particular area, local media *is* thinking big. If you're trying to build a million-dollar business or a global brand, you've got to get outside of your own backyard.

The best way to get started is with research. Find someone who's been in your position, maybe even someone who's in your industry and shares your area of expertise, and see where they have gotten press. Then, see what journalists/ producers cover that beat, whether it's lifestyle, tech, or something else. A lot of these reporters and producers are on social media, and some of them even post calls for stories.

Get on their radar by interacting with them on their social channels (like, comment). Then, you are not just another name when you pitch them.

When you send a pitch, make sure that it's customized to the journalist who is going to receive it. Be clear about the value that your story will bring to their audience. That means you must do your research first. Sending one pitch to the right person will yield much better results than sending a hundred pitches to the wrong people.

One of my clients went from being on local press to appearing on national news.

Pam Robinson had done very little media when I started working with her. She was going through a bad divorce and was down in the dumps. She and her girlfriends decided they wanted to feel like kids again and just have fun. They started, on a regular basis, getting together and doing Double Dutch jump rope. Then other friends started joining. Next thing you know, it went from three of them to six, and so on.

The way it rapidly expanded became a really good story. She didn't see it. She thought she was just taking care of her mental health. "That's what journalists are looking for," I told her. "They're looking for stories that audiences can relate to."

We got her featured in a local community newspaper. And her next step was *CBS Mornings* national news. That exposure helped her increase her visibility exponentially, and she now has thousands of members all over the world. Pam now runs a nonprofit, The 40+ Double Dutch Club, dedicated to the value of fun, fitness, and friendship.

A good story is what opens doors and attracts media opportunities. See what you are bringing to the table, hone in on your real value, and make it into a story with mass appeal. That's the golden ticket. It'll be a boon for your business.

> Stacia Crawford is an award-winning PR and media strategist with more than thirty-five years of experience as a television news producer. She helps authors, entrepreneurs, and industry leaders share their messages on TV, radio, and in magazines so they can increase their authority, influence, and income. StayReadyMedia.com.

CHAPTER 36:

Underpromise and Overdeliver in Any Media Situation

KAT NEFF

In any career, there's this baseline of expectations. Be professional. Meet your deadlines. Do good work.

For any book, service, product, or business promotion, there's expected marketing. And there's going above and beyond.

When you "underpromise and overdeliver" in your media activities, it allows you to shine, while making the host look good. Plus, the audience/reader/prospect gets the benefit of your knowledge. It's the ultimate win-win-win.

Once you get booked as a guest on a podcast, video interview, or TV show segment, there are certain things you can do to get the most out of the experience.

Craft questions and talking points. Put together a list of preferred interview questions that you would like to be asked.

Not all hosts will request this, but it never hurts to have it. This enables you to focus on the information that you think is most beneficial to the audience. While you're at it, send over your preferred short bio, a current headshot, and your social media links for them to follow, tag you, and share. You may also want to write up how you want to be introduced.

Research the show and host. In a perfect world, you are a long-time fan of whatever show you are going to be on. If that is not the case, make sure you watch, or listen to, several episodes, so you are clear on the run of show, tone, and demographic. Also, do basic research on the host to discover what's near and dear to their heart. For example, if the host is involved with environmental causes, find a way to incorporate it into your conversation. When you connect with them beyond the subject matter, it builds rapport and makes you memorable.

Rehearse. Record yourself being interviewed and play it back. Think about ways you can be less nervous, be more compelling, and surprise the audience with your unique, personalized take on the subject matter.

To underpromise and overdeliver means to do anything and everything you can to make the host or producer's job easier. You also want to present the heck out of your subject matter. It's the best way to make an impression and get a return invitation.

Kat Neff has more than twenty years of experience in the mind/body/spirit genre of book publishing. She has helped countless authors achieve national and international media bookings by creating successful broadcast, online, and print media publicity. Kat is also a frequent speaker on various aspects of book publishing. KatNeff.com.

CHAPTER 37:

Remember Hanlon's Razor

MARK HERSCHBERG

"Never attribute to malice that which can be adequately explained by stupidity."

—Robert J. Hanlon

So often we get bad information or are let down by coworkers or others. Sometimes it can feel like they actively undermined you. More often than not, they are doing the best they can, just like you, but their assumptions, constraints, knowledge, and/or understanding led them to take a well-intentioned action that may seemingly do more harm than good. It's best to assume good intentions and get to the bottom of it, rather than go into conflict mode from the start.

Once, in a nonprofit I volunteered with, some students asked me to confirm an event so they could book a nonrefundable flight. I checked with my supervisor and she confirmed it, so

I confirmed it to them. Two days later, I got an email from my supervisor that the event was off. The students probably thought I was an idiot or never bothered to check. But clearly, I had. I might think my supervisor didn't check, but she may have, too. Heck, the event may have been on two days before, but then a disaster impacted the facility through no fault of anyone's.

Ultimately, it's better to initially assume good intentions and bad luck than a hostile act. Only if it happens repeatedly should you question the reliability of the other party.

> Mark Herschberg is a CTO, MIT, instructor, author of *The Career Toolkit: Essential Skills for Success That No One Taught You*, and creator of the Brain Bump app. TheCareerToolkitBook.com.

CHAPTER 38:

Add Your Personality and Spin

JEFFREY EISNER

Every time I get a new idea, the first thing that I do is evaluate how I can make it different, so it stands out.

When the Instant Pot came on the market, it burst onto the scene hard-core. Every recipe creator was trying to jump on that bandwagon, due to the popularity. I started at the beginning too, so I got in there at the right time.

If there's a trend going, and you know it's going to be of use to people, you want to figure out how to put your own spin on it. But there are only so many content creators that people are going to follow. You need to stand out from the rest.

Do you remember the trend of recipe videos that were like montages? They ran about thirty seconds; the food looked great, and it was shareable content. But you had no idea how to prepare the dish.

I'm very much a visual person. I like to teach that way. And I am going to hold your hand through the process. I'm basically your friend in the kitchen.

My method and approach to cooking also incorporates my own schtick—I'm from Long Island, and my accent gets much higher and thicker when the cameras are rolling. My content will help you whether you're a person who's never cooked a day in your life or a seasoned cook. I just want to give people information that's useful.

I am also prone to follow people who lean into their personality, like Maangchi, who is like the Queen of Korean cooking. She's fabulous! There are other people, like Ina Garten, who is so soothing to me. I'll do anything Ina wants me to do.

By adding your voice and your face to your content, you make yourself different and stand apart from the rest.

My passion was always to cook and to help people, and I've married those two things in a way that is approachable. It started out as a side thing. I was working in a job that I didn't enjoy, as a video content producer for blue-chip clients. I would go home and use cooking as my therapy. That was my thing.

I started my Pressure Luck Cooking YouTube channel to show people how easy mac and cheese is to make. That got me excited; I had a passion for it. Did I know anything would come of it? No. And I had no plan. I just wanted to do something that made me happy.

Yes, it's great to have aspirations, set goals, and work toward them, but at the same time, don't set expectations too high. At the end of the day, you have to be doing it for you.

This sounds cliché, but follow the advice of Glinda from *The Wiz*: "If you believe in yourself, you very well might be onto something really, really great."

Life is too short. If you are not happy with what you are doing with your life, and feel your talents can be used elsewhere, use your time and focus on something else.

We all need a paycheck; we have to live. But there's always a way to apply your skills to something you are happier doing. I was a video producer. And now I am my own one-man video team. It is a bit much sometimes but allows me to keep everything very organic and real.

The three takeaways are:

- Set yourself apart; be different.
- Give the people something that can be of use to them.
- Do it for yourself above anything else.

If you believe in yourself—that you have something good going—and it can be of use to other people, that's when things start to take off.

You might become a bestselling author and write five books in five years. You might end up on *Rachael Ray*. You might end up on the Food Network with three professional chefs cooking alongside you, and you're sweating bullets the entire time and providing the episode's comic relief.

When you have a little bit of personality and pizzazz to go with your passion, who knows what could happen!

> Jeffrey Eisner is the number one bestselling author of the *Step-by-Step Instant Pot* series of cookbooks. His newest, *Pastabilities*, is his fifth cookbook. Featured on the Food Network, *Good Morning America*, and as a frequent guest on *Rachael Ray*, he creates famously flavorful recipes in the bustling city of Queens, New York. He also loves pinball and theatre. Check him out at PressureLuckCooking.com and on the various social media platforms.

BONUS CHAPTER:

Effective Communication Is About Feeling, Not Thinking

RICHARD WALTER

Intellect, logic, and reason occupy a critically important place in our personal and professional lives.

Creativity, however, resides elsewhere.

To succeed in any enterprise—financial, commercial, artistic, or educational—you do not need to make people feel good, but merely feel.

If you provoke them, upset them, make them weep, scare them half to death, they will follow you to the ends of the earth.

Instead of transmitting data, tell a story.

Some instructors say the one thing you should *not* do is write your own personal little story. Nobody cares about that.

I say, you should *only* write your personal story. No matter what you write, it's going to be personal because you're not an android, you're not a machine. Even when you share other people's stories, they will be filtered through you—your lens of experience. And that's what will get people to connect with you.

Many years ago, a friend of mine—another long-time professor at UCLA, except he retired from the School of Public Health, not Film—was writing a book about alternative health care. He said, "You're a writer. Take a look at this." He had a draft ready, hoping for a publisher.

It opened with something like, "Alternative health care methodologies and modalities have arisen in the last several years. In this book we're going to take you through its evolution, starting with acupuncture." And blah blah this and blah blah that.

Eventually, he got to the part where he talked about how his child had suffered severe burns in a household accident. Then he shared everything his family had gone through to find the right treatment for his son. I told him that those are the details that people will care about, not numbers and statistics.

We've all heard the expression "Beware my foolish heart."

In fact, it's the head that's foolish. The heart is smart.

Richard Walter is an author of bestselling fiction and nonfiction, celebrated storytelling educator, screenwriter, script consultant, lecturer, and retired professor who led the screenwriting program in the film school at UCLA for several decades. His latest novel, *Deadpan*, was published in 2024 by Heresy Press. RichardWalterBooks.com.

PART 6 -
PRODUCTIVITY

You can't add more hours to the day. You can develop habits that lean into your availability, tendencies, and strengths.

CHAPTER 39:

Paper for Productivity

CHRISTOPHER MCKENNEY

I am very traditional; I use paper to write down and track my goals. I have my good old yellow pad, which I use to set my goals every day and every week, and I keep a journal with larger, longer-term goals.

For me, using paper is analogous to my preferences in reading. If I try to read an ebook and then take a test on it or try to be part of a book group discussion, my comprehension levels are just not the same as with paper. It has to do with the stickiness of that information.

I have used a tablet in the past; the Remarkable tablets tend to be really good for sketching out wild scenarios and brainstorming. But, as a tool, I find a good old pad of paper keeps me in a very tactical-execution mode. And then I write love notes to my future self in my long-term journal. These two "tools" help me manage my projects and responsibilities.

Plus, I love the dopamine hit of being able to cross things out. Maybe other people do, but I don't get the same feeling if I'm doing that in some software package or on my Remarkable tablet. I typically update my yellow pad every two days, as I am managing multiple scenarios. Things get resolved and priorities change. I can cross off certain elements, revise them, or revisit them later in the week.

As someone who loves tech, and spent years immersed in Silicon Valley, I have a bit of an oddball perspective.

I see tech as a set of tools. These can enhance what we do in our work and personal lives, as long as we do not use them as a crutch or an excuse. I understand the gaming mentality and being able to level up, and all of that. But for me, when I've used various project-management or goal-setting software packages, their "gamification" of goal setting and execution tends to become the purpose, rather than being the tool used to achieve that purpose. Like many people, I will set up all sorts of bells and whistles, reminders and notifications, and it's great that the software can do all that. But meanwhile, I've just spent a lot of time overdoing that process, when it takes me two minutes to update my paper lists.

Achieving your goals is all about incremental action; it's what you do every day to make things a little better. It's like the magic of compounding interest. When you manage it on paper throughout the year or several years, you can really see progress. It's astounding!

Christopher McKenney is the founder and CEO of Mango Publishing Group, an innovative book publisher based in Miami. Winner of many awards, including #1 Fastest Growing Publisher by *Publishers Weekly* two years in a row, Mango is helping to reinvent book publishing. In his over thirty-year career, McKenney has worked in corporate publishing as well as participated in two other publishing technology-based startups. Chris earned a BA in History from Brown University and received an MBA from UCLA. He is married to the Pulitzer Prize-winning journalist and editor Mary Rajkumar, and they have two children. MangoPublishingGroup.com.

CHAPTER 40:

Wear One Hat at a Time

CYNTHIA KORTMAN WESTPHAL

I learned a while ago that I am much more productive when I wear one hat—one identity—at a time.

I've got the mom hat, the wife hat, the friend hat, and, for a long time, I had the taking care of aging parents hat. I've been a professor at a university for twenty years, and I just took over as chair of that department. Plus, I have an online company that I co-founded, where I manage a team of twelve, so I am an entrepreneur, content creator, and online teacher. I've also continued to work professionally as a freelance musician for Broadway shows, tours, and regional productions, and I'm director of one summer theatre camp in Michigan, and on faculty at another camp in Oklahoma. So I'm juggling a number of job hats, plus the personal hats.

When I first started my career, I focused on being a Broadway musician. For ten years, I worked exclusively on Broadway, music directing, conducting, and playing keyboards for shows such as *The Lion King*, *Miss Saigon,* and *Fascinating Rhythm.* For a long time, I didn't think I wanted to get married or have kids, but that changed in my thirties, and it took me a while to figure out how to manage all of the new hats!

I'm definitely led by a sense of purpose, as well as my curiosity. If something sounds interesting to me, I tend to find time to do it. However, this only works when I don't try to do everything at once.

In the beginning, I would be at home with the kids (mom hat), trying to do email (work hat), while trying to listen to them tell me a story. Or I'd be out of town working but get distracted because I felt guilty about missing my mom activities.

That never went well.

If I'm trying to toggle back and forth between three work email addresses or five projects, I'm going to half-ass all of them, and feel overwhelmed at the same time. What I've learned is to put on one hat at a time and set aside the others. That way, I don't have the guilt or that nagging feeling that I should be doing something else, because I know I'll get to it, and when I do, it'll get my full focus.

Setting timers helps me commit to one identity at a time. I make it a game and a challenge for myself by setting weird times, like forty-three minutes. And, when the timer goes off, I move on to something different.

Staying focused on one identity at a time helps me be much more efficient, more organized, and more present with the people and the work that I love.

> Cynthia Kortman Westphal is chair of the Department of Musical Theatre at the University of Michigan, where she has taught since 2004. While on sabbatical in 2018–19, she music-directed the first national tour of the Tony-winning production *Come From Away* with her family in tow. Broadway credits include *The Lion King, A Christmas Story, Miss Saigon*, and *The Gershwin's Fascinating Rhythm*, as well as over a dozen Broadway national tours. She developed new musicals with Glenn Frye of the Eagles and Graham Russell of Air Supply, and toured with opera superstar Andrea Bocelli.
>
> Cynthia is a certified master teacher in Estill Voice Training, is the co-founder of Broadway Vocal Coach, and serves as co-host of the *Broadway Vocal Coach* podcast. She serves as a mentor for both Maestra, an organization that provides support to the women and nonbinary musicians in musical theatre, and MUSE: Musicians United For Social Equity. Bwayvocalcoach.com.

CHAPTER 41:

Baby Steps Every Single Day

HOLLY HOMER

I wish I had a fancy way to say this, but the bottom line is: make "progress" every day. I use quotes around the word progress because progress isn't always progress in the right direction, but it is momentum. Course correction is easier when you are at least moving. It often feels like just doing one or two things (sometimes in just ten minutes or so) won't make a big difference, but combined, over years, it can build an empire.

There are other benefits to working on your business (or anything) over time. Those simple steps you took three years ago might not have been effective, but what you learned may be the foundation to something that you can use today. Everything happens for a reason, and the more we pay attention to that, the more we can leverage our experience to take it to the next level.

When I started blogging twenty years ago, I had never written anything. I was a physical therapist and spent time in labs, not creative writing classes! I decided that I would write every day, which I did, until one day I went to bed without putting in the work and felt bad about it. So bad that I woke up in the middle of the night because of a storm and ended up at my computer, staring at a blank screen. With the thunder and lightning outside the window, I wrote a short blog post, inspired by the stormy night, hit publish, and went to bed.

When I woke up, I was embarrassed about the silly stuff I'd written the night before and decided I would go delete it before anyone read it. Imagine my surprise when I opened up my blog to multiple comments and two personal emails about how that blog post was the best thing I had ever written! I challenge that, but I would have never written it in the first place if I hadn't pushed myself to take action daily.

> Holly Homer accidentally started a blog twenty years ago and hasn't stopped. She runs KidsActivities.com and is a co-founder of Pagewheel.com, which makes life much easier! She lives in the suburbs of Dallas with her husband, three boys, and a Frenchie named Panda.

CHAPTER 42:
Lists, Batching, and Boundaries

PAULA RIZZO

When I first started working for myself after years as a television producer, I was overwhelmed and exhausted. I realized I needed to do the things that had helped me be productive for nearly twenty years in television news: lists, batching, and boundaries.

Having a list by my side at all times is like having a roadmap. I know what my intentions for the day are and what is coming up next. This is very important, no matter what industry you work in, but it was particularly helpful when working in media. Things changed fast, and I needed to keep track of everything in one place. I still make my lists the same way I did then—at the end of the day. I look ahead to the following day and write out everything that has to be done the next day. That way, when I get up and start my day, I know exactly what has to happen, even if something else distracts me.

I also batch all like tasks and meetings together whenever possible, and it makes a world of difference. Just as you wouldn't do your laundry one sock at a time, the same goes for paying bills or doing Zoom calls. I also set strict boundaries around when I'll do meetings—both times and days of the week. This way I can make sure I'm not tired and overcommitted.

This is how I structure my week:

- I keep Monday clear of meetings and use it for getting ready for the week and doing any writing assignments that need to be done that week.
- Tuesday through Thursday is when I schedule meetings with clients or media.
- And Fridays are reserved for creative writing. It's how I wrote my second book, *Listful Living,* and how I finished my novel as well.

I also will only do meetings at 11:30 a.m. or 1 p.m. ET if I can help it. This keeps balance in my day and allows me to have a lunch break and not get cranky.

This all matters to my business and productivity. It will help yours too!

> Paula Rizzo is an Emmy Award-winning television producer, bestselling author of *Listful Thinking* and *Listful Living*, media-training coach, speaker, LinkedIn Learning Instructor, host of the live-stream show *Inside Scoop*, and creator of the popular online training *Media-Ready Author*. She also writes a regular column for *Writer's Digest*. Grab Paula's free guide, *10 Media Questions Every Author Needs to Answer*, at PaulaRizzo.com/10q to create buzz for your book.

CHAPTER 43:

Give Yourself a (Lunch) Break

EITAN BERNATH

I like to 100 percent turn my brain off when I eat lunch, so that I can laser-focus when I am working.

Throughout the day, I try to maximize every second. I find that it helps my focus, during lunch, to turn on some type of television show. This is something I do almost every day. I put my phone on "do not disturb," and I put away my smartwatch and computer. That way, I don't get distracted during this downtime.

I don't even take a half an hour or hour lunch break; I probably take about fifteen minutes. For me, that's enough. Once I'm done, I feel rejuvenated.

For example, today, I had seven cooking videos on my slate to film. I filmed three, and put on some music while I prepared lunch. I then put my phone away, turned on *Veep*, and watched about fifteen minutes; I was dying of laughter. And then I got the rest of my filming done. I even finished early.

As a chef/entertainer, I do not watch cooking TV at lunchtime. I specifically watch comedy. I also find that, once I get that break out of my system, I feel less inclined to play on my phone—scrolling through social media, watching a random TikTok video—for a few minutes here and there.

A lot of times, we grab our phones and just mindlessly scroll, because our brain needs a break. I find that giving my brain a complete break in the middle of the day negates my need for short bursts of zoning out.

> Eitan Bernath is an award-winning chef, author, TV personality, entertainer, and social justice activist. His entertainment career began at just eleven years old, as one of the youngest-ever contestants on Food Network's *Chopped*. Since then, Bernath's social media presence has amassed over eight million followers, three billion annual video views, and annually reaches more than 350 million people in 150 countries. He is the CEO of Eitan Productions, the Principal Culinary Contributor for the Daytime Emmy® award-winning *Drew Barrymore Show*, and is a contributor to *The Washington Post, Food & Wine, Saveur,* and *Delish*. Bernath's 2022 debut cookbook, *Eitan Eats the World*, is a national bestseller. EitanBernath.com.

CHAPTER 44:
Schedule Time to Work

JASON FALLS

One thing that has kept me both productive and sane is blocking time on my calendar to work. It's important to insist that you are not available for meetings or conference calls, or even emergencies, in those time periods. The majority of today's business world can be best summarized in one word: "meetings." And the more you have, the less work gets done.

Plan for time to work and defend that time on your calendar. You'll maintain productivity, not have to take as much work home, and thus protect your work-life balance and—bonus— you won't have to attend as many meetings. "I'm not available then," is a perfectly professional response.

I developed the rule when I was embedded in a large corporation as a consultant. I was contracted to work for this company for twenty hours per week. I had back-to-back meetings from eight a.m. until two p.m. Monday with an hour for lunch (five hours), then three hours of standing meetings on Tuesday, Wednesday, and Friday (nine hours).

That meant I only had six hours per week to get work done, and the project I was leading required focused work for at least ten to twelve hours per week.

I explained the math to my client contact/supervisor and asked them to pick the four to six hours of meetings each week I could be excused from. Otherwise, I would have to redefine the scope and charge more for my time. It worked, and I was excused from all but two meetings per week. I kept up with the topics, thanks to a post-meeting email that bullet-pointed the subject matter. When I had questions, I followed up in less than ten minutes and saved the client thousands of dollars in unnecessary costs for me sitting and listening to three departments argue over whose budget things should or shouldn't come from.

> Jason Falls is a digital marketing consultant, author, and podcaster specializing in influence strategy and social media intelligence gathering. He authored the first-ever conversation report using social media data for consumer insights in 2016, as well as bestselling business books on social media and influence marketing strategy. Falls is an adjunct professor of communications at the University of Louisville, executive producer of the Marketing Podcast Network, and an Americana music aficionado. He also abhors meetings. Find him online @jasonfalls or at JasonFalls.com.

CHAPTER 45:
Calculate the Consequences

PETER SHANKMAN

Whenever I have a choice to make, I ask myself, "How am I going to feel in twelve hours?" I call it the twelve-hour advance rule. Some people call it "playing the tape forward."

For instance, if I get invited to a party, I'll ask myself, "Do I want to go out tonight, where I don't really know anyone, just to say I went? Or do I want to get a good night's sleep and get up early and exercise?"

Allowing yourself to see the future in twelve-hour increments enables you to make better-informed decisions.

"Seven p.m. Peter" wants to go out and have fun. He also knows that if he goes to that party, when the alarm wakes him to exercise, "four a.m. Peter" is not going to be happy. "Four a.m. Peter" has to live with the consequences of "seven p.m. Peter's" actions.

Thinking like "four a.m. Peter" at seven p.m. allows me to analyze the outcome in a different way. That has helped me tremendously when it comes to setting goals or getting things done that I need and want to get done.

Let's say I have a project deadline. Instead of going out, I can start working on it, knowing that once I have made a big dent in it, that will make it easier to finish. If I procrastinate, I'll be thinking about it until I start working on it the following night, which may stress me out and impact my ability to focus on other things.

It's a know-thyself thing. It's much easier for me to live my best life by *not* doing certain things.

There's a great line in the movie *War Games*, which came out in 1983, with Matthew Broderick. The computer learns that there are no real winners in the game of nuclear war. The last line of the movie is the computer saying, "It's a strange game. The only winning move is not to play."

I've learned in my life that there are several situations where the only winning move is not to play. So, I don't play. And if that means I don't go to a party, or I don't stay out late at night, and instead get a good night's sleep, that works for me.

> *The New York Times* has called Peter Shankman "a rock star who knows everything about social media and then some." He is a six-time bestselling author, entrepreneur, and corporate keynote speaker, focusing on neurodiversity in the workplace, customer experience, and the new and emerging customer and neurodiverse economies. With four startup launches and three exits under his belt (most notably Help a Reporter

Out), Peter is recognized worldwide for radically new ways of thinking about customer experience, social media, PR, marketing, advertising, and neurodiversity. Founder of SOS (Source of Sources) fourteen years after selling HARO to a major media company, Peter is back to his roots, having launched SOS to again help connect journalists with sources. Peter is the Futurist in Residence at Price Benowitz and BluShark Digital and is a worldwide influencer for several global brands including Adobe, Sylvania, National Car Rental, Manscaped, Thule, and many others.

Peter is a single dad, a two-time Ironman triathlete, and a class B licensed skydiver, and has a pretty serious Peloton addiction. When he's not traveling around the world speaking to companies big and small, he's based in NYC, where he was born and raised, with his eleven-year-old daughter and three-year-old rescue dog, both of whom consistently refuse him access to his couch. Shankman.com.

BONUS CHAPTER:

Catalog Your Ideas

KATE WOLIN

I've had a very nonlinear career path, and part of that is because I'm super-curious. There's always something interesting that I'm pulling a thread on. It used to be that I would get an idea and, because it was only half-baked, I wouldn't even write it down. It would get lost.

I found a way to keep these fleeting thoughts top of mind, so they can develop organically into something amazing.

I keep a stack of three-by-five index cards in every purse, every bag; I know this is very old school. And whenever I hear something interesting or I have a new idea, I write it down. Then, when I hear something that connects to it a couple weeks later, I just add it to the card.

As an introvert, and as a scientist, I have this aversion to self-promotion. So, having a system for cataloging ideas about my expertise and my interests enables me to develop them in a way that feels authentic. And, because I am keeping track, these random ideas end up evolving into something down the line, whether it's a class I decide to teach, a webinar I offer to lead, or a blog post that I write.

For instance, I work in digital health, and one of the things that happens a lot with tech solutions—in healthcare and other areas—is that people will download an app and never open it. Let's say someone has a family history of heart attacks and needs to build a physical activity routine as part of their cardiovascular disease prevention goals. If I'm trying to help someone manage a chronic condition, I need them to download the fitness app and consistently engage with it.

The concept is broadly called engagement, and it is frustrating to me that people talk about engagement in this generic, blunt way. When you need someone to engage with your app every day, every week, for a month, six months, a year, forever, there's a lot of nuance. I needed to find a solution to this puzzle, to help people get invested in that process.

For months, I had "What is engagement?" on my index card. This idea kept swirling over my head, kind of like Pigpen in the *Peanuts* comic strips with dust following him everywhere. I would look at the notecard, wondering, "Do I have anything else to say about this? What do I want to say about engagement?" I got very frustrated, because I couldn't figure out what I really wanted to say. Still, I would look at the card every day, hoping something would click.

It finally did! I read something, somewhere, that helped me solidify my thinking. As a result, I wrote this blog post about what our field gets wrong about engagement. Funnily enough, it had the highest engagement from readership I had on a post in years. New people came into my network and wanted to have conversations. It got cited by others who were struggling with the same thing. It brought in a new job opportunity for me and a consulting engagement.

Even more importantly, this clarity allowed me to move on. Once I figured out what was puzzling me, and I turned it into something, it created the headspace I needed so I could go explore something else.

> Dr. Kate Wolin is a behavioral epidemiologist, digital health entrepreneur, investor, and professor. Following her academic medicine career at Washington University School of Medicine and Loyola University, Kate co-founded and served as CEO of a digital health startup that was acquired by Anthem, Inc. She then served as Chief Science Officer of a population health platform company and as head of product for Optum's direct-to-consumer business.
>
> Dr. Wolin is an advisor to startups and enterprise organizations on bridging clinical and behavioral science with commercial product strategy and execution. She is an investor in early-stage digital health companies. Kate earned her doctorate at the Harvard School of Public Health and completed her fellowship training at Northwestern Feinberg School of Medicine. She is currently on the entrepreneurship faculty at the Kellogg School of Management at Northwestern. She has been named as a *Forbes* Healthcare Innovator That You Should Know and a Notable Woman in STEM by Crains, and Dr. Wolin is a Fellow of the Society of Behavioral Medicine and the American College of Sports Medicine. DrKateWolin.com.

PART 7 -

LEADERSHIP AND TEAMWORK

Whether you are a business owner, artist, or thought leader, you will likely need to work with others in order to achieve a common goal.

CHAPTER 46:

Let Your Team Know They Matter

CHEF SUSAN FENIGER

As a leader and an owner, it's essential to have communication and respect for the people who work for you, whether it's the dishwasher or the CEO. Having the people in your orbit feel respected, listened to, and seen is really important. That also has to do with the customers who are coming in, but that sort of happens naturally.

Within our restaurant, the people here need to feel that they're respected for who they are, that you care about them and that, if there's a problem, there's an open door. The result is they get the best from you and you get the best from them.

When we opened Alice B. I was in the kitchen, not because our chef really needed my help; I was in there to show support. I was in there, peeling ginger, peeling garlic, and chopping onions. I would be there as early as he was, at seven in the morning, and until we closed around ten at night. I would go over to help the pot washer do pots and pans, because I feel like that sends a message, which is that, if the owner can do that, then that person's part of our team.

We had this woman the first week, who didn't speak any English; she was very shy and sort of giggly, and she was doing pots and pans. She said to someone to tell the chef that she had to leave by nine o'clock, and he was sort of like, "You never said that when we hired you." We told her, "We need you to be here till at least 10:30," and so she stayed.

For the next two or three weeks, every day, I'd make a big deal of saying, "hello," to her, and making sure all the servers and the kitchen people knew who she was. As each week went on, she got more and more comfortable in what she was doing. Then, whenever she had a little bit of a break, she started doing some prep work. You could see she was good, so we kept giving her more and more responsibilities. Now, she's no longer a dishwasher; she's making all the biscuits daily and she knows the recipes by heart. She's speaking a little bit more English and is way more confident.

Someone else who worked for us had a similar success story. By focusing on her and giving her a sense of confidence—helping her feel like she was seen—she ended up becoming our lead pastry person.

This woman walked in off the street—this is downtown LA—with zero experience. I was up in the attic cleaning and the chef told her if she wanted a job, she could help me clean. This woman had a silk shirt on and long fingernails; that didn't stop her from helping me. She came back the next day, and we did it again. The following day, we hired her as La Tortillera (the tortilla maker). She ended up moving into pastries and doing the pastries for us for the next ten years.

Work with the people on your team and get to know them. That's a rule I think every business owner should have.

> Susan Feniger is a chef, restaurateur, cookbook author, and radio and TV personality. She is known for starring in the cooking show *Too Hot Tamales* and *Tamales World Tour* on the FOOD Network, *Iron Chef*, *Top Chef Masters*, *Cooking with the Master Chefs*, and more. For forty years she has traveled the world, bringing food from different cultures back to her several influential Los Angeles restaurants, Ciudad, Street, Border Grill, and Socalo, introducing Angelenos to authentic global dishes.
>
> She has received a Lifetime Achievement Award from the California Restaurant Association, the *LA Times* Jonathan Gold Award celebrating intelligence, innovation, culture, and environment, and the Julia Child Award honoring an individual who has made a profound and significant difference in the way America cooks, eats, and drinks. Learn more at BorderGrill.com and ForkedtheFilm.com.

CHAPTER 47:

Managing Down Is as Important as Managing Up

ED BRILL

Leaders create cultures that engage project teams and bring out the best in individuals. Managing down means treating everyone as a valued, respected member of an organization, surfacing their expertise, advocating for their ideas, and removing blockers that inhibit progress. Yes, that sounds like management 101, but the specific focus is applied to the notion of servant leadership.

By investing more of a leader's energy in elevating their team members, the leader in turn is elevated by demonstrating the organizational commitment and effectiveness to get stuff done. This approach works because employees row boats in the same direction, rather than competing for scarce resources (including the time and attention of their boss), contribute peer-level recognition more freely, and seek to bring their best selves to work every day.

During my time as Vice President of Information Technology at IBM, the CEO asked our team to convert the entire company onto a brand-new product. We had nine months to deploy to 500,000 end users globally. The product was so new that it didn't actually work for the first two weeks of the rollout. Due to the tight timeframe—yes, nine months is fast for a company-wide project!—I inherited an existing project team and basically was told to make it work.

The first few weeks were chaotic, as we tried to simultaneously learn, plan, and act. I realized the team needed safety above everything else. They needed to know that failures with the product were not their fault or responsibility, and that they could make mistakes in this uncharted territory.

About six weeks into the project, I brought the whole team together in a windowless conference room in New York City. At the start, they were told, "This is the worst day of this project. Every day from here forward we will work together, and we will get better, and we will be successful."

We spent the next two days building trust and confidence, brainstorming ways to accelerate the project, and identifying norms and communication tools. As the leader, my promise was that I would always have their backs, and that it was more important to me that I listen to them than to the three people above me on the corporate ladder. Those people were my customers, but this team were the experts.

We managed to finish the project within budget and a month ahead of schedule. It was one of the best technology rollouts that ever happened inside IBM, with a greater than 99 percent success rate. And it all happened because the project team knew they were being given the room to do what they needed without typical distractions, drama, or judgement.

> Ed Brill is Managing Director of Desert Ridge Solutions, a boutique management and technology consultancy. His corporate career included multi-decade leadership of IBM's Collaboration Solutions portfolio and CTO/Chief Product Officer roles at several industry-focused technology organizations. DesertRidgeSolutions.com.

CHAPTER 48:

Mentor Your Replacement

BRENDA KNIGHT

If you have lofty goals for your career, one of the best things you can do is identify, hire, and mentor your own replacement. This is something you can do, whether you work for other people or you have struck out on your own. The latter appears more obvious; you want to have someone to carry on your business and legacy. The former is also important.

Whatever your career, when you are ambitious, you likely have your eyes pinned to the next step or milestone: position, job, or company. I feel like it's a counterintuitive tip, but I think it's a very practical.

Early on in my career at HarperCollins, there were many opportunities. It was a multinational company, so you could leap to another state, country, or division. Ideally, you've downloaded your skills, knowledge, wisdom, and tips—basically your brain—to a team member, associate, or even an intern. That way, when you need to move up or move on, it's not a hardship for your company or team.

Whether you work for a small business, a mid-sized company, your own company, or a multinational corporation, you need to be protective of every aspect of your role. This includes the big picture, the small details, and the team. Making sure everything is covered also makes you the ideal employee for your next opportunity.

I often say I want to end my career working for one of my interns. It is kind of a joke, but I'm actually serious about it. I have had three interns in the last fifteen years, who were remarkable young women. I was absolutely blessed and honored to get to work with them.

At this point in my career, I feel I'm like a Jedi warrior and my interns are my Padawans. Some years down the road, I will want to hang up my lightsaber. My Padawans will become the Jedi warriors, doing the good work and fighting the good fight, and training the next generation.

> Brenda Knight is Publisher of Mango Publishing Group and the Founding Editor of the Books That Save Lives imprint. She began her career at HarperCollins, working with luminaries Paolo Coelho, Marianne Williamson, and His Holiness the Dalai Lama. Knight is the author of *Random Acts of Kindness*, *The Grateful Table*, and *Women of the Beat Generation*, which won an American Book Award. Her recent book, *Badass Affirmations*, has sold 350,000 copies. She serves as President of the Women's National Book Association, San Francisco Chapter and resides in the SF Bay Area. She blogs about acts of kindness at LowerHaightHoller.Blogspot.com.

CHAPTER 49:

Seek Alignment

KEITH SPIRO

My go-to business rule is to only accept projects where there is personal and professional alignment.

When I feel alignment with an organization's goals, and their leadership reciprocates with equal passion and commitment, I know that I will be able to help accelerate success. I seek their team's like-minded attention to detail, and curiosity to test, experiment, and pivot with my guidance. I am engaged to organize people power, align resources, and build communities of allies and supporters.

Imagine a group of more than a hundred volunteers working together to build, mostly by hand, a reconstruction of the first ocean-going English-built ship in North America. Add twenty years of sweat equity, and the result is a twenty-first-century operative wooden ship with a seventeenth-century spirit and core. I came aboard to share the story with a wider audience while inspiring accelerated growth. The goal was to rally a wide range of divergent interests to make this unique organization successful.

The nonprofit Maine's First Ship launched the pinnace *Virginia* on June 4, 2022. In June of 2023, it arrived at Boothbay Harbor's Maine Windjammer Days as both the oldest and newest member of the fleet. Folks in Bath, Maine, lovingly refer to the organization as the second most active shipyard in town.

This organization is dedicated to exploring history, celebrating ingenuity, and building community. These three pillars are their foundation for future growth. They continue to gain support by adding more docents and maritime makers to the growing team of volunteers. Interested parties, both near and far, are welcome to "Join the Crewe" in a very hands-on way.

At the end of 2023, I received a thank-you note from Maine First Ship's Executive Director, Kirstie Truluck. Her words validated why I found this project so engaging and meaningful.

"A great group of board and committee members have been activated in a joyful way. And you have helped make it all possible. It is clear to all [at this company] that your generous spirit and infectious energy and curious nature make us better, month by month and year by year."

When I feel that a team, looking to hire me, matches my energy and spark, I am all in. The process begins with meeting people where they are, learning about their motivations and passions, while looking for alignment of people and mission.

If you are not excited about, aligned with, and enthusiastic for a project's mission or company vision, ask yourself if it is worth your time, energy, and attention. Remember, time is the most precious resource we have. To joyfully activate a whole organization guarantees success. Align well and accelerate the team to their success.

> Keith Spiro is a business strategist and community builder with a keen interest in working with high-impact startups and other organizations that can make a difference in community and health. He has deep experience in both large corporate and small or nonprofit business sectors. Learn more at KeithSpiroMedia.com.

CHAPTER 50:
Understand the Business Side of Your Creative Process

BARBARA LAZAROFF

I was one of seven women who founded an organization called the International Association of Women Chefs and Restaurateurs in 1993. I had already opened Spago Hollywood in 1982, as well as Chinois in Santa Monica, Eureka in West LA, Granita in Malibu, and a few other restaurants. However, I was the only restaurateur (and designer) who was not a professional chef among the group.

A number of years ago, at the annual conference of the WCR, I had the pleasure of speaking with an aspiring baker in one of the smaller work group sessions. This young baker expressed the desire to open her own donut shop. While I wasn't a baker, I was certainly becoming a seasoned businesswoman.

"That's wonderful," I said. "I appreciate people who really know what they want and work hard to achieve it." Then, I asked, "Do you have any idea what it costs your boss to make each item?"

She looked confused and asked me to explain.

"Do you know the cost of the flour, the sugar, and the other ingredients? Do you understand how much labor/time goes into making each donut?" She did not.

The last thing I wanted to do was discourage a young person, but I believe when you give advice, you need to be helpful and explicit.

"If you want to open a business, you likely need to raise money," I said. "If you need to raise money, you need to know your costs."

While the specifics vary for different businesses, every business needs a plan.

I suggested she continue working with "XYZ Bakery"—I knew its reputation—and learn all she could.

I also told her that the business plan needs to consider not only the cost of producing the product, but the location costs, operational costs, licenses, insurance, and many more details, like how you differentiate and promote your product.

Social media wasn't as prevalent as it is today, so we talked about more traditional means of getting your business noticed, including small charitable events. Clearly her visibility opportunities would be greatly aided these days by social media campaigns.

"This sounds overwhelming now," I said, "but as you research this, bit by bit, you will have a clearer overall picture of what it takes to start a bakery."

Costing a product is a sum of many fundamentals in business. Spago is more expensive than many other restaurants, but we don't utilize any frozen items—only fresh, high-quality organic produce, and very select meats and fish. Our staff, from the chefs and the line cooks to the servers, are paid very well for their talents.

Additionally, all businesses have expenses that much of the public doesn't really think about, such as liability insurance, building maintenance, utilities, and much more, referred to as overhead and operating expenses. A restaurant, large or small, is a complex package of parts, which of course includes the more obvious, food and labor. All of that is factored into how much we have to charge for a product.

We have earned our visibility and reputation over more than forty-two years, so we spend less on publicity, but we do allocate some funds to social media and branding. When we first open any business, there is also some money in the budget for contingencies (unexpected costs) and some working capital (if the business doesn't generate revenue right away).

Also important to note: there's the value of your product or service and the "perceived value." Your customers want to believe your product is worth what they are paying. In our case, we like to think of our restaurants as an event, and always hope to exceed those expectations! It's up to you, the business owner, to give your customers/clients an overall experience that makes them feel that way.

This is relevant for products as well, whether it is a donut, a beauty product, or a candle!

Let's say you are selling hand-made candles. Your costs are also going to include the packaging, which sometimes might be more expensive than the candles themselves.

Focus on the quality of your product first. However, realize you also need to consider the packaging, the time factor, any additional labor, if you have a staff, and other costs, such as shipping. Then extrapolate the costs over volume.

If you don't know how to figure out your costs and need help making a business plan, find people who have done it before. I suggested that the young baker take a business class at a community college or online, go to a conference, and/or seek out mentors. She actually called me a few times—I was happy to help and set her up with one of my pastry chefs to talk about types of ovens and brands of flour.

Especially if you are just starting out, ask someone you admire for a favor, a tip, or an idea. In most cases, they'll be more than happy to share their wealth of knowledge with you. As we climb the ladder of success, I always say, reach back and take someone's hand!

Barbara Lazaroff is both a highly regarded restaurateur and notable commercial designer, renowned for her innovative restaurant concepts. She is member of the American Society of Interior Designers (ASID) and owner/president of Imaginings Interior Design, Inc. She is also a producer, writer, published author, celebrated philanthropist, humanitarian, and entrepreneur. Barbara is the co-founder of the Wolfgang Puck Brand, and is co-founder of the restaurants Spago, Chinois, and CUT, among other restaurants, having created many of these spaces. She is also co-founder of Wolfgang Puck Worldwide, which includes the company's licensing. BarbaraLazaroff.com.

CHAPTER 51:

The Buddy System

LISA M. GILFORD

One thing that I've found essential, no matter what I'm trying to achieve, is that I don't go it alone.

I'm a partner at a law firm, and part of my job requires bringing in clients. It is a major measure of success in my position and in my profession. Just as it is easier to sell the services of a friend than it is to sell yourself, it's much easier to pitch as part of a team. When you present to clients and prospects, having support and backup in the room gives you an advantage.

Whenever I start preparing a pitch in an effort to get new business, I begin by figuring out who I would hire if I were the client. What expertise do I need to complement my own? I then create a pitch, using the resources of my group of trusted peers and partners. We all have different backgrounds, experiences, and perspectives, which is what makes these kinds of collaborations so powerful.

While that is one very specific example, I think that applies to pretty much everything. I often rely on information, support, and resources provided to me through my network, whether I'm working toward a professional or personal goal. Using a buddy system somehow makes whatever it is that I'm doing a little easier and a lot more effective.

Lisa Gilford is a leading complex civil litigator with a practice focused on class actions, multi-district litigation, product liability matters, and large-scale commercial disputes. Lisa co-chairs Sidley's Diversity Committee in Los Angeles. Lisa's numerous accolades include being named by the Los Angeles *Daily Journal* as one of its "Top 100 Lawyers" (2015–2020), "Top Women Lawyers" (2013–2019), and "Top Women Litigators" in California (2013–2018). The *Los Angeles Business Journal* named her to the "LA 500" (2019, 2020), as one of the city's "Most Influential Women Attorneys" (2018–2020), and among the "Most Influential Minority Lawyers" (2019).

Dedicated to causes advancing the status of Black women and girls, Lisa is a former president and current Emeritus Board Member of the National Association of Women Lawyers. She serves on the Board of Directors of the NAACP Legal Defense and Education Fund; is a former member of the boards of the California Women's Law Center and StepUp Women's Network; a lifetime member of Women Lawyers of Los Angeles and Black Women Lawyers bar organizations; and counsel to the S.H.A.U.N. Foundation for Women and Girls and the Debbie Allen Dance Academy.

Lisa earned an LLM from Georgetown University, a JD from the University of Southern California Gould School of Law, and received a BA from Furman University (1990).

CHAPTER 52:

Successful Projects Are a Combination of Hard Work, Creativity, and a Positive Attitude

DYLAN KENIN

When working with others, show up with the understanding that everybody is there to get ahead or reach a goal. It puts you in a better frame of mind to succeed collectively.

For a film or TV show, producers and directors assemble teams. The whole pre-production process is, "Let's get the best people we possibly can." At no point are they going, "Let's just hire somebody who is good enough."

Film sets can be very tense places. There are always limitations—time, budget, and expertise—but it is such a creative medium. Every person there is creative, from the directors and actors to the grip and the gaffer.

Take the lighting people, for example. The lights need to be set up in a specific way. The person has to get the cable from the generator to the five-hundred-watt light across a sound stage, which is littered with carts and people and equipment. So that person has to get creative about how they run that cable. They come to work very early, leave work very late, and spend the whole day doing a pretty thankless and difficult job. And that's a person whose name you never read in the credits, because you got up and left the theatre before their name came up on the screen.

You have the makeup artist who's rushing in to touch up their lead actor before the camera starts rolling. They didn't get the five minutes that they needed to put her lip gloss back on, so it would match the previous shot. The assistant director is yelling at the makeup lady, "What are you doing in here?" And she says, "I'm trying to do my job." The makeup artist has been told by the script supervisor that the actor's lip gloss has to match the last setup. For whatever reason, it's important in this scene. And the AD says, "Well, do it faster." It is his job to make sure that everything *does* run faster.

A film set, like any project, is such a symbiotic machine. When somebody is *not* doing their job, it becomes evident pretty quickly, and that person is let go. Things need to be done in order and done right, so the final product is the best it could be.

Show up, assuming that everybody is there to elevate the project; everybody wants you to do your best work. I truly believe that one of my best attributes is a positive attitude. It shows in the process and in the final project.

As far as my own career goes, most of the time, when I leave the set, people go, "Man, we're so glad you were here. Thanks for bringing that energy." In fact, one thing that does happen to me quite a bit is that I end up getting jobs through referrals. A lot of the time, when somebody says, "Oh, I've got an actor for that," it's not because we're best friends and not because we keep in touch, though I try. More often, somebody had a good experience of working with me, and that kind of word spreads.

Everybody having a better time in the present leads to more people thinking about me in the future.

> Dylan Kenin was born in a small town in New Mexico and had big dreams of storytelling from a young age. In high school he was awarded a National Merit Scholarship and used the opportunity to move to Los Angeles and pursue a degree in theatre from University of Southern California. He has been working in the industry ever since.
>
> Dylan has been featured in quite a few projects you're probably a fan of and many more you've never seen. Be your own judge by checking out his imdb.com. Some of the influential filmmakers Dylan has worked with include Denis Villeneuve, Stephen Gaghan, Antoine Fuqua, Andrew Niccol, and David Mackenzie, as well as Seth MacFarlane, Joseph Kosinski, and Taylor Sheridan, to name just a few. His hobbies include meditating, motorcycling, woodworking, collecting life-long friendships, and never giving up.

BONUS CHAPTER:
Sustainability First, Scalability Second

TROY SANDIDGE

Growth is a byproduct of maintaining a consistent level of success that gradually increases while meeting the same level of effort-to-result ratio simultaneously. This practice works because it ensures your effort, energy, risk, and cash flow are not extended beyond what is manageable. This also forces you to face your reality and gauge your success based on concrete OKRs (objectives and key results) and KPIs (key performance indicators) that matter specially to your livelihood and not what the market is projecting or others are achieving. It keeps you honest. And businesses built on truth are easier to be agile with.

Most businesses fail simply because of lack of money. They had a great idea, a solid industry, and the only reason time was running out was because their money ran out. So, the optimal way to be successful is to achieve sustainability first, as a constant always, and anything extra can be focused on scaling and expanding.

I was advising a tech startup during the pandemic to prioritize sustainable growth, trying to test and define themselves in the marketplace over chasing immediate hyper growth to appeal to current investors or attract new ones too quickly over one big brand choosing to use them. I emphasized the importance of building a viable product and a stable business model before scaling too aggressively.

In their first year, though very reluctant with so much hype and press, they followed the advice. By focusing on refining their flagship offering to meet market demands, they were able to deliver value to a variety of customers. And even though their growth might not have been as rapid as some other startups, they maintained a steady pace and avoided overextending themselves and were able to build a cushion to employ staff for better infrastructure and customer success.

Ultimately the results were significant. They built strong pockets of business in industries even after the pandemic and didn't fall once the pandemic external effects went away. They had built a loyal customer base and set a strong foundation for future growth better than many of their peers who prioritized hyper growth but faced instability and had to pivot or stop.

Troy Sandidge, a.k.a. the Strategy Hacker,® is a global speaker, growth marketing strategist, award-winning podcaster, and author who builds sustainable, scalable, and profitable strategies, systems, and solutions, generating over $175 million in client revenue and successfully launching over thirty-five brands worldwide. FindTroy.com.

CONCLUSION:

What's Your Secret?

Whether you read the book straight through or tuned into the parts you needed, we hope you are feeling inspired, motivated, and ready to take action.

Here are your next steps:

- Make a note of the tips that resonated with you.
- Try them out.
- Identify which activities and strategies best help you stay focused, boost your well-being, take action, grow your network, communicate more effectively, improve productivity, and enhance your leadership/teamwork skills.
- Adjust, adapt, and incorporate these ideas into your routine.
- Keep going! You've got this!
- Stay in touch. We'd love to know what you are working on and what works for you, so we can cheer you on.

Share your experience through the Facebook group: Facebook.com/groups/52Secrets and/or using the hashtag #52secrets or #52secretsbook on social media.

Also, visit 52SecretsBook.com for news, events, videos, bonus tips, more resources, and information on the themes for future books.

Do you have a secret to share? Check out our guidelines at 52SecretsBook.com/Submissions. You could end up in a future edition of *52 Secrets*.

AFTERWORD:
Embrace the Grit Mindset

GUY KAWASAKI

I don't approach goals in a formal, organized, or maybe even rational way. I decide to do something, and I keep at it. For me, it's all about the grit mindset. As my wife has told me, "You are a dog with a bone." I take a big bite, and I won't let go. On the other hand, if I don't care about something, nothing can make me want to do it.

I took up hockey at forty-four and surfing at sixty, because my kids took up hockey and surfing, and I wanted to join them. I don't do anything halfway, either. I built a backyard rink, and I do a lot of dryland training for surfing. When I get an idea in my brain—for instance, that I want to be a decent surfer or a decent hockey player—I go all in.

That being said, I am not a believer in the concept of work-life balance. I think that, over your lifetime, you can balance out the work and the life, but, at any given moment, you cannot have fifty-fifty. When you're younger, you give up on your life part and work your ass off. And then, when you're my age, you can focus on your life and work a lot less. Over the course of my life, if you add it all up, I hope it's around fifty-fifty, but, at any given moment, it's seventy-thirty, or thirty-seventy.

As far as my interests are considered, often things find me. Podcasting found me when I was on a book tour. I took up writing, because I wanted to put out a book that documented my feelings about the Macintosh Division. I'm living my life, and if something strikes my fancy, I embrace it and apply a lot of grit.

There's an old Chinese saying that you have to wait by the side of a river a very long time before a duck flies into your mouth. The duck doesn't fly in your mouth, you've to go get it, cook it, and then eat it.

> Guy Kawasaki is the chief evangelist of Canva and the creator of Guy Kawasaki's *Remarkable People* podcast. He is an executive fellow of the Haas School of Business (UC Berkeley), and adjunct professor at the University of California, Santa Cruz and the University of New South Wales. He was the chief evangelist for Apple and a trustee of the Wikimedia Foundation. He has written *Think Remarkable*, *Wise Guy*, *The Art of the Start 2.0*, *The Art of Social Media*, *Enchantment*, and eleven other books. Kawasaki has a BA from Stanford University, an MBA from UCLA, and an honorary doctorate from Babson College. GuyKawasaki.com.

APPENDIX A:

Learn More About...

Here's Where to Find Everyone Who Shared a Secret in the Book

Patrick J. Adams: SuitsSidebar.com and follow @PatrickJAdams on Instagram

Alex Amouyel: Get in touch or follow her on LinkedIn

Jeff Bajorek: JeffBajorek.com

Angela Miller Barton: Wellcoaches.com

Eitan Bernath: EitanBernath.com

Dave Bricker: Speakipedia.com

Ed Brill: DesertRidgeSolutions.com

Howard Brown: ShiningBrightly.com

Bobbie Carlton: CarltonPRandMarketing.com and InnovationWomen.com

Chef Katie Chin: ChefKatieChin.com

Magie Cook: MagieCook.com

Stacia Crawford: StayReadyMedia.com

Kevin Daniels: Follow @KevinDaniels27 on Instagram

Jess Dewell: RedDirection.com

Wendy Diamond: AnimalFair.com and JoinWEDO.org

Heather Eck: HeatherEck.com

Jeffrey Eisner: PressureLuckCooking.com

Jason Falls: JasonFalls.com and MarketingPodcasts.net

Chef Susan Feniger: BorderGrill.com and ForkedtheFilm.com

Amy Ferris: Facebook.com/amy.ferris

MJ Fievre: MJFievre.com

Lisa M. Gilford: Sidley.com/en/people/g/gilford-lisa-m

Jeff Goldberg: JGSalesPro.com

Greg Grunberg: TalkAboutItOnVideo.com

Elaine Hall: Elaine-Hall.com and TheMiracleProject.org

Liz Heiman: RegardingSales.com

Mark Herschberg: TheCareerToolkitBook.com

Holly Homer: KidsActivities.com and Pagewheel.com

Christina Toy Johnson: ChristineToyJohnson.com

Guy Kawasaki: GuyKawasaki.com

Dylan Kenin: IMDB.com/me/dylan

Brenda Knight: LowerHaightHoller.Blogspot.com

Liz Lachman: LizLachman.com and ForkedtheFilm.com

Barbara Lazaroff: BarbaraLazaroff.com

Michael Lennox: MichaelLennox.com

Larry Levine: SellingFromtheHeart.net

Chris Levinson: Find on IMDB.com

Christopher McKenney: MangoPublishingGroup.com

Dr. Jaime Moriguchi: CalHeart.org

Kat Neff: KatNeff.com

Jamie Pachino: JamiePachino.com

Jeff Pulver: Pulver.com

Paula Rizzo: PaulaRizzo.com

Michael Roderick: SmallPondEnterprises.com

Jessie-Sierra Ross: StraighttotheHipsBaby.com

Chef Rossi: TheRagingSkillet.com

Dave Sanderson: DaveSandersonSpeaks.com

Troy Sandidge: FindTroy.com

Peter Shankman: Shankman.com

Arthur Smith: ASmithCo.com

Mari Smith: MariSmith.com

Keith Spiro: KeithSpiroMedia.com

Dayna Steele: DaynaSteele.com

Tracie Thoms: Follow @TracieThoms on Instagram

Brynne Tillman: SocialSalesLink.com

Viveka von Rosen: BeyondtheDreamBoard.com

Richard Walter: RichardWalterBooks.com

Jennifer Watson: StormFrontFreaks.com and @JenniferWeather on Instagram/TikTok

Cynthia Kortman Westphal: Bwayvocalcoach.com

Dr. Katie Wolin: DrKateWolin.com

APPENDIX B:

What Is the DEB Method?

The DEB Method is my brainstorming and task-based system, designed to help you figure out what you truly want, so you can make a plan to turn your dreams into reality. The ultimate goal is to live a happy, fulfilling life. And that starts with gifting yourself the time to decide what that means for you. I say that the DEB Method is "goal-setting simplified," because changing your life is challenging enough. I made the instructions really easy.

DEB stands for **D**etermine Your Mission, **E**xplore Your Options, **B**rainstorm Your Path. The first part of *Your Goal Guide* goes into the DEB Method in detail. Here's an overview of how my approach works.

Determine Your Mission

To get what you want, you need to know what that is. Whether you are looking to start or grow a business, change careers, elevate your expertise, or achieve work-life balance, setting goals starts with knowing what you are seeking.

Start with Visualization

When you close your eyes and think of the life you want, what does that look like? Are you a sought-after speaker? Bestselling author? Respected business owner? Model employee? Enjoying a happy personal life?

Start with the picture in your head. Then, create a visual representation. Draw a picture, go old-school (get out those crafting supplies), or create something electronically.

For instance, if you want to be listed on a *Forbes* Top Ten list, go into Canva or your favorite graphics app, and mock something up. Seeking a new job? Create a certificate declaring you "Employee of the Month" at your dream company. If you are aspiring to travel, take a family photo and place it in your desired location.

Use your visual representation as a screen saver or your phone background, or keep it on your desk, where you will look at it regularly. Eye on the prize.

Write Your Current Biography

You probably already have some form of a bio, but does it really lean into who you are and how you want to be known?

Unlike a resume, your bio is written in narrative form, in your tone and style, and in the third person. It can run from a few lines or a couple paragraphs to a page or two. Your bio combines your accomplishments, experience, and expertise with your strengths and values. It's a good reminder of all you have to offer, as well as a way to take inventory at the starting point of your goal journey.

To make you more memorable, throw in some unique facts. A version of mine says, "I believe in cooking for productivity, dancing for exercise, and talking for fun."

Having trouble writing about yourself? Try crafting your bio after attending a networking event, when you have just introduced yourself a bunch of times. Or ask friends and peers for their impressions of you. They probably have some great perspective and will be happy to help you out.

Predict Your Future Biography

Your future bio has two purposes: it reinforces the visualization exercise from the first step, while inspiring you to keep moving forward.

Obviously, the details will likely change—your *real* future hasn't happened yet. A future bio is another way to zero in on where you are going and what you desire to accomplish. You can write your future bio geared toward the end of the year; one, five, ten years from now; or all of the above; that's up to you!

Like the current bio, your future bio needs to be written in the third person and in the present tense. Include awards and milestones; you can even put in personal aspirations. Add your headshot and mock it up like a magazine article or book cover bio, and you can turn it into your visual representation.

Have fun with it! There are no limits.

Create a Mission Statement

When you work on anything, do so with purpose. It fuels your journey.

Your mission statement is a summary of what you do, as well as the driving force behind your goals. It combines who you are (your biography and your values) and what makes you unique, along with your main intention and how you help. To "help" can be to entertain, inform, educate, or make someone's life better through a product or service.

Who Are You + What You Want = Your Mission Statement

- **Who are you?** What is your work, education, and personal background, as it relates to your ultimate goal?
- **What are your values?** What ideals and principles are important to you?
- **What are your unique qualities?** What characteristics, talents, and skills don't just describe you, but define you?

- **What do you ultimately want?** What is your big, long-term goal?
- **Who does it serve and why?** What is the value to others? *This still works for personal goals. For instance, if your goal is a healthier lifestyle, it will impact your family and work in a positive way.*

For instance:

- Professional: "I am a (adjective) person who enjoys (talent) and excels at (skill) who wants to help (demographic) (do this) in order to (reason)."
- Personal: "I am a (adjective) person who does (skill), enjoys (interest), and wants to do (action) in order to (do this)."

Write Your Motto

A mission statement tends to be long and detailed; a motto is a short, pithy phrase that embodies who you are, along with your purpose.

On any goal journey, you want all of your activities to relate to or reflect your mission. Your motto can be a tagline, slogan, theme song, title, anything. It is a shortened version of your mission statement that acts as a guide.

As potential opportunities come your way, you can look to your motto. "Is doing this in alignment with my goals?" If yes, then go for it. If no, then ask yourself, "Would it have other benefits? Will it be a good networking opportunity, a much-needed break, or something fun?" If yes, then yes. If no, then you also have your answer.

Use your motto to keep you motivated and focused as you assess what is in line with your goals, what has value in other ways, and what you need to avoid altogether.

Explore Your Options

Once you have zeroed in on your ideal life, it's important to take the time to figure out what steps to take to turn it into reality. Whereas Determining your Mission sets the foundation for your goals, Exploring your Options is the research phase. It helps you delve into all the possible paths ahead of you.

Directed Journaling

Directed Journaling is my brainstorm-based approach to identifying the projects and pursuits that are the most meaningful to you and will best support your aspirations.

Have you ever noticed how difficult it is to figure things out by simply rolling things around in your head? This strategy is effective, because when you put your ideas in writing, you are able to look at them objectively and make a decision about the best course of action.

Here's how it works:

- Set up a series of ten- to fifteen-minute appointments with yourself; schedule three, four, or five of these over the course of the week.
- During these sessions, write down your thoughts—through stream of consciousness—on a specific topic. Ask yourself questions, such as "What kind of business or side hustle do I want to build?" "What project can I create to express my thought leadership?" "How can I advance in my career?" "What new career would be the best use of my skills and experience?" Or simply "What's next?"

Your journaling can be narrative, a list, an outline, phrases, free-writing, drawing, or all of the above. You can even dictate these ideas and put them on paper using a voice-to-text program. The trick is to let everything out of your head, related to something specific. No editing, no worrying about repeating yourself. Just a pure, unadulterated free-writing. Then, you can use that information to craft your plan.

Do not look at your brainstorms until after you've done them a few times. You'll see what to do with this information in the next step.

List Common Themes

The reason I tell you to not look at your writing until you've completely finished your rambling is so you can approach your ideas objectively. You want to find the commonalities.

Read through everything once. Then go back through your journal entries. Using a highlighter, or by writing things down in a separate notebook, note the ideas you mention numerous times. You may have thought you knew exactly what you wanted to pursue, but you only mentioned it twice. Something you may have considered a whim you wrote paragraphs about in every session.

Need to change your employment situation? You may be able to determine whether you need to find a new position at your current company, make a lateral move to a different company, or explore another career path.

Looking to start a business? This will help you hone in on your industry or specialty, as well as what type of business: service or product, online or offline, full-time or side hustle.

Want to become known as an expert? Discover the best way to showcase your knowledge, whether it's through a book, a podcast, videos, social media posts and photos, speaking, or a combination.

Do you want/need a more balanced life? Identify what that means, what's holding you back, and which changes you can make to your current situation. This could be related to yourself, your home, family, or friends.

The ideas that capture your attention deserve the most consideration. That is where you will put the most energy.

Identify Options

From your notes, choose ten options that embody your mission and motto. Then narrow it down to five. You can always go back and explore more, but this will get you started.

Answer the following questions about your top five:
- Why does this interest me?
- How will it serve my mission and motto?
- In what ways would it be a good fit?
- Which of my experience and skills can I use to pursue this?
- What additional education, support, and resources will I need?

From this information, you should be able to narrow your options down to three finalists. These are the ones you will zero in on.

Research the Possibilities

When exploring potential endeavors—considering a new job or career, launching a business or side hustle, writing a book, or starting a podcast—you want to gather enough information to be realistic about what you might be getting into, but not so much that you get overwhelmed.

By doing research up front, not only will you tap into what excites you, you will be better equipped to make a plan. Start with reading books and articles, listening to podcasts, watching videos, and joining online and real-life communities and meetups. Then, reach out to your network: your connections *and* your connectors—the people who may not have the information you need, but always know someone who does.

See if these friends, peers, and others, who have the information you seek, are open to having an in-person coffee, phone call, or online conversation. Ask questions, take notes, and be sure to thank them for their time and see if there is something they need.

Select Your Primary Goal

After doing the legwork, you likely have enough information to choose which goals to pursue.

Before you commit, however, ask yourself these questions of your top three possibilities:

- Does this choice match my original vision?
- Is it aligned with my mission and motto?
- Does it support my objectives?
- What, if any, adjustments will I need to make to my life/schedule to pursue this?
- Do I *want* to do this?

While you want to make certain your goals align with your mission and vision, it doesn't need to be 100 percent on everything. If you are excited about the path ahead, 90 percent may be good enough. As long as you end up happy, living your ideal life, that is what matters.

Remember, this is written in ink, not stone. You can always go back and explore other options. Just be sure to give any pursuits enough time to make a concerted effort.

Brainstorm Your Path

Goals work together and build upon each other. Long-term goals are comprised of short-term goals, short-term goals are made from benchmarks (milestones), and benchmarks are comprised of tasks (action items). Brainstorming your Path is about taking all of these elements and creating a plan that sets you up for success.

Brainstorm All Goals

You know how sometimes less is more? With brainstorming, more is more. You want to write down everything you think is relevant to any and all of your goals. This includes easy goals, realistic goals, and dream goals.

Make a list of all of your:

- Personal and professional goals
- Short- and long-term goals
- Simple action items and tasks

- Anything you want to do or have been meaning to do

Your master list can be on paper, electronic, or both, which is what I do. Use a notepad for your master list. Then type it up. You will come up with things you may have forgotten the first time around. Plus, a digital list is easier to organize.

Once you get your goals out of your head and onto the page, you can start categorizing them.

Organize Professional Goals

The next step is to divide and conquer. Separate your master list into two categories: professional goals and personal goals. Group similar items together. *We will address your personal goals in the next section.*

Take your list of professional goals and identify which are the long-term goals.

- Write each long-term goal at the top of a new piece of paper or document.
- Put any short-term goals from your list under the appropriate long-term goal.
- Add benchmarks under each short-term goal. These are mini-hurdles.
- Under each benchmark, write out the tasks necessary to accomplish it.

Most of the items will come from your master list, while others will occur to you during this process.

Organize Personal Goals

Personal goals complement professional ones. When you do things to improve your personal life, it impacts your career and vice versa. Personal goals, whether they are related to projects or lifestyle changes, should be treated with the importance they deserve.

Project-based personal goals can be mapped out and managed the same way you navigate a professional goal. Lifestyle personal goals are more ongoing and less structured. Since they tend to be pursued in a more organic way, these can be accomplished simply by changing your routine.

For lifestyle goals, make an extensive list of all the necessary action items. Then set aside time each day or each week to work on them. For instance, if the goal is to spend more time with your family, make a list of the activities everyone likes to do. Then set aside one afternoon or evening each week for family time, when you participate in one of the activities.

Prioritize

The more goals, benchmarks, and action items you have, the easier it is to narrow them down and prioritize.

From your extensive list, choose three of the long-term goals. One of these may be a dream goal, but the other two can be more realistic. Remember, long-term goals can take one to five years or so. Next, choose three long-term personal goals. These will likely work in concert with your professional goals. Now hone in.

Choose three short-term professional and three short-term personal goals. Short-term goals can take one to three or six months, though sometimes longer. These are the goals you will pursue as you strive to achieve your long-term goals.

Choose Alpha and Beta Projects

Even though you prioritized, you can't possibly do everything simultaneously. This is especially true if you, like most people, already have a slew of other obligations: day job, social life, family.

Choose one primary and one secondary project to work on in tandem. Feel free to mix and match your professional and personal goals. When you have two projects in motion—whether they are directly aligned (developing a product while creating a website for it) or not (looking for a new job while prioritizing healthy lifestyle changes)—it keeps you moving forward. If you get stalled or need a break from your main project, you have another one prepped and waiting in the wings.

Your goals, your life, your choice. Go on out there and go for it. We know you can do it!

For more on the DEB Method, including worksheets, exercises, examples, and resources, get a copy of Your Goal Guide: *A Roadmap for Setting, Planning and Achieving Your Goals.*

P.S.: THANKS FOR READING

I truly hope you got a lot of value from reading this book. I would love to stay connected.

Join the Facebook group: Facebook.com/Groups/52SecretsBook

Submit your secret: 52SecretsBook.com/Submissions

Email Deb@TheDEBMethod.com

Find me on LinkedIn.com/Coastbunny

Learn more about *GoalChat* and read the recaps: TheDEBMethod.com/Blog

Follow @TheDEBMethod on Facebook, YouTube, and Instagram

Subscribe to *GoalChat* and *Taste Buds with Deb* on iTunes or your favorite podcast platform

Join Facebook.com/Groups/WriteOnOnline and Facebook.com/Groups/TasteBudswithDeb

And, if you found *52 Secrets for Goal-Setting and Goal-Getting* helpful, I would love it if you would consider leaving a review on Amazon, Barnes & Noble, or Goodreads. Thanks!

To your success!

ACKNOWLEDGEMENTS

You can't reach your goals on your own. You need your people.

Thank you to my family, friends, communities, mentors, peers, and clients. Thanks to my agent, Paul S. Levine, and to Chris McKenney, Brenda Knight, Robin Miller, Roberto Nunez, Nathaniel Parker, and the wonderful team at Mango Publishing.

And thank you to all of the experts I interviewed for this book. I loved our conversations and truly appreciate you taking the time to share your secrets.

ABOUT THE AUTHOR

Debra Eckerling is on a mission to change goal culture in and out of the workplace.

She is the author of the award-winning *Your Goal Guide: A Roadmap for Setting, Planning and Achieving Your Goals* (Independent Publisher Book Awards, Silver Medalist, Self-Help 2021) and creator of The D*E*B Method, which is her system for goal-setting simplified. DEB stands for Determine Your Mission, Explore Your Options, Brainstorm Your Path. You can't get what you want unless you know what you want. Creating a foundation for your personal and professional goals sets you up for success.

A born connector, motivator, and facilitator, Debra has a knack for bringing parts of a project, people, and communities together. Her expertise has illuminated the path for countless individuals globally. She has assisted them in areas ranging from penning books, crafting book proposals, and launching blogs to strategizing business projects and figuring out work-life balance. She has also served as a consultant and workshop facilitator for businesses and teams, offering goal-setting, personal and professional planning, content development, event strategy, and team-building.

Debra has spoken on stages for TEDx, Innovation Women, Lioness Magazine, VON, Agorapulse, TechMunch, California Creative Writers Conference, LA County Bar Association Lawyer Well-Being Project, Women's National Book Association, where she serves on the board as Networking Ambassador, and more.

A freelance food, lifestyle, and business writer, Debra contributes to *First for Women*, *Woman's World*, *Writer's Digest*, and the *Jewish Journal of Los Angeles*. However, nothing makes her happier than being in front of the microphone. She is the host of #GoalChatLive a.k.a. *GoalChat* on the Marketing Podcast Network and hosts the award-winning *Taste Buds* with Deb podcast on the *Jewish Journal* podcast network. Subscribe to the videos @TheDEBMethod on YouTube and the podcasts on iTunes and/or your favorite podcast network.

Mango Publishing, established in 2014, publishes an eclectic list of books by diverse authors—both new and established voices—on topics ranging from business, personal growth, women's empowerment, LGBTQ studies, health, and spirituality to history, popular culture, time management, decluttering, lifestyle, mental wellness, aging, and sustainable living. We were named 2019 *and* 2020's #1 fastest growing independent publisher by *Publishers Weekly*. Our success is driven by our main goal, which is to publish high-quality books that will entertain readers as well as make a positive difference in their lives.

Our readers are our most important resource; we value your input, suggestions, and ideas. We'd love to hear from you—after all, we are publishing books for you!

Please stay in touch with us and follow us at:

Facebook: Mango Publishing
Twitter: @MangoPublishing
Instagram: @MangoPublishing
LinkedIn: Mango Publishing
Pinterest: Mango Publishing
Newsletter: mangopublishinggroup.com/newsletter

Join us on Mango's journey to reinvent publishing, one book at a time.